KEW
ON A
PLATE
WITH
RAYMOND
BLANC

KEW
ON A
PLATE

WITH

RAYMOND
BLANC

RECIPES, HORTICULTURE AND HERITAGE

TEXT BY **SHEILA KEATING**

headline

CONTENTS

IN A UNIQUE COLLABORATION between the Royal Botanic Gardens at Kew and double Michelin-starred chef Raymond Blanc, a corner of the historic 300-acre site has been transformed into a stunning walled kitchen garden, the like of which has not been seen at Kew since Georgian times. Planted with heritage varieties of fruit and vegetables, many with their own evocative histories, the garden has provided a sumptuous source of inspiration for Raymond's collection of seasonal recipes, bursting with colour and flavour.

'Just getting back in touch with the natural cycles of the year, getting your hands into the dirt and growing something that you can cook for your family and friends to enjoy is immensely good for the spirit and the soul,' says Kew's Director of Horticulture, Richard Barley.

❛ The creation of the garden with Raymond and his team has been a wonderful opportunity to remind us all of the joys of growing and cooking our own food, and to show how aesthetically beautiful fruit and vegetable gardens can be', says Richard Barley, Kew's Director of Horticulture. 'In many ways we are repeating Kew's history on this patch of ground, which was once an extensive, productive kitchen garden for the Royal Palaces. Several of King George II and Queen Caroline's family lived in the Palaces, including eldest son and heir Frederick Prince of Wales and his wife Princess Augusta (who founded the botanic garden). King George III, who spent much of his childhood at Kew, later returned with Queen Charlotte and their extensive family. Melons were grown in an area that is still known as the Melon Yard – along with newly fashionable pineapples and other exotic fruits. At the same time, Sir Joseph Banks, the adventurer, botanist and unofficial director of Kew, who sailed with Captain Cook on his epic voyage to the south Pacific and Australia, was creating an international centre of plant study, collecting samples of fruits and vegetables from all over the world. These were meticulously studied, logged and preserved, and cuttings and seeds were freely given to market gardeners to popularise.

The kitchen garden project has also reinforced the very real link between Kew's research into plant diversity, chemistry and genetics, and the day to day hands-on growing of food, whether that is in a plot in the back garden, on an allotment or smallholding or on a global agricultural scale. It is a connection that is becoming increasingly important as we seek to understand and manage the world's ecosystems and feed the expanding population while our climate is changing. There are potentially 50,000 edible plants in the world, yet we know that around half of the global food intake is based on just four crops: rice, wheat, soy beans and maize. What would happen if one of these four key crops were to fail completely?

In past centuries, people knew better how to live locally off the land; they had a keener sense of seasonality and a diet that varied according to whatever was available. Now, we expect to be able to buy anything at any time of the year, but the large scale, intensive production of food and its transportation around the world which has made that possible have also brought with them problems: pollution, degradation of the soil, water shortages and the destruction of ecosystems. These are all serious challenges for modern society, and our scientists are now working to find ways to secure the future of our food supply.

Particularly important is Kew's Crop Wild Relatives programme. In partnership with around 50 similar organisations around the world, our scientists are involved in finding, collecting, studying and conserving the seeds of the wild cousins of 29 of our commonly cultivated crops. These wild relatives are so much more genetically diverse and hardy than today's more nurtured, cultivated crops, and many have specific traits that enable them to be grown in difficult conditions. They can be used to develop new varieties which can be grown by local communities, which will be much more suited to particular microclimates and resilient to pests and diseases.

All of this links directly to the need to get back to producing more of our food locally, and even better, growing some of it ourselves. The fruit and vegetable garden at Kew is testimony to the pleasures of fresh, seasonal food, which, of course, is the hallmark of Raymond's brilliant recipes. It is doing something very valuable in focusing on selected heritage varieties that have often been edged out in commercial growing by modern hybrids, but that can sometimes deliver much more characterful flavours. By helping to perpetuate these varieties we are contributing to conserving the all-important biodiversity.

What we hope is that the new garden will not only help visitors to think about the bigger picture, but at a local level inspire them to rediscover the simple pleasure of planting, growing and harvesting, in however small a way. You don't need an acre of ground; it is amazing what you can produce in a few square feet, or in pots on a balcony or patio. Just getting back in touch with the natural cycles of the year, getting your hands into the dirt and growing something that you can cook for your family and friends to enjoy is immensely good for the spirit and the soul.❥

'I absolutely love gardens,' says Raymond Blanc. 'After all these years I am still in awe of their mysteries and complexities. I marvel at the life cycle of a seed as it grows and responds to the iciness of winter and the heat of the sun; the deep understanding of the gardener, waging constant battle against winged insects, caterpillars, furry creatures, blight or mildew; and the extraordinary rhythm of the seasons, which mirrors and defines our own lives and has always been at the heart of my cooking.

The rhythm of the kitchen garden, with its seasonal changes, has always been at the heart of Raymond Blanc's cooking.

As human beings have done for millions of years, we long for the first pale sunlight of spring, warming the earth, encouraging the first shoots to come through, giving us beautiful, delicate flavours, colours and blossoms and the first asparagus, radish or pea shoots. Next, the ripeness of summer with its triumph of full-flavoured abundance, so that the cook is totally spoilt. Then autumn, rude and ripe with the big, rich colours of plums and apples and pumpkins. And afterwards comes the slow decay and collapse into winter with its black earth, seemingly barren, but in reality full of the seeds of new life, while through the frosts and snow the cabbages and leeks and Brussels sprouts come surging defiantly through the soil.

I gained a deep affinity with the seasons, the garden and of terroir from my father, and a love, care and understanding of cooking and preserving food from my mother. We lived in the most rugged, wooded part of France with mountains, rivers and lakes; warm in summer but freezing in winter. It is a terrain where intensive farming cannot thrive, so there is still purity in the fruits and vegetables that are grown, and the organic values I have always embraced were instilled in me early on in life. My father created a huge garden where we grew enough food for our family of seven. While my friends were playing football, me and my two sisters and two brothers were digging the soil and turning the compost, watering and harvesting food for my mother to cook, bottle or pickle to store for the winter. So although I cannot say I am a gardener, I certainly served my apprenticeship.

When I arrived at Belmond Le Manoir aux Quat'Saisons, the first thing I did was to create the vegetable garden, even before I worried about the house, the foundations, the roof or the decor – and now we have 11 different gardens and orchards, inspired by my travels, my own terroir, books I have read and marvellous people I have met. So why did I want to make another garden at Kew? Well, of course I relished the idea of a French Republican laying a new garden of 250-strong varieties over a former royal plot! But seriously, what is beautiful is that after a gap of more than 150 years since the last royal kitchen garden was given up in Victorian times, vegetables are being grown again in this part of Kew. It has been an amazing chance to show that there is a real connection between rediscovering, valuing and growing traditional varieties of fruits and vegetables on a local scale and the much bigger, complex and challenging question of what the world is going to eat tomorrow. This is where the great work that is being done by the scientists at Kew, the pinnacle of plant research, is so very important.

When we talk about heritage or 'heirloom' varieties we mean plants that have been grown and their seeds saved and replanted for centuries. Each has its own individuality of flavour and character and over time the plants have naturally adapted themselves to local conditions. Modern hybrid seeds, which are known as F1, on the other hand, have usually been developed for their enormous yield, resistance to disease, shelf life and perfect colour, shape and uniformity. Many certainly grow bigger, but they have less and less taste. And they are designed to be used once only. If you were to try to harvest their seeds and grow them the next year, the crop wouldn't be the same, so you will always have to buy more. And if an entire crop should fail, what are you left with when these hybrids have replaced so many alternative heritage varieties? I am not saying that heritage varieties are necessarily best, but many are, and it is vital that we don't lose them – not only for their flavour and character, but for the biodiversity they bring, which is so important to our future food security. We believe that plenty is going to be forever, but our world is so vulnerable and our food supplies so fragile.

'I am not saying that heritage varieties are necessarily the best', says Raymond, 'but many are, and it is vital that we don't lose them – not only for their flavour and character, but for the biodiversity they bring, which is so important to our future food security.'

I have a deep respect for science, especially as a self-taught and curious cook; I always wanted the mysteries of the kitchen explained to me. I needed to know why my soufflés rose beautifully or why colours, textures and flavours denatured through the appliance of heat. I had to understand the whole chemistry of the fermentation of yeast in bread. And I truly believe that scientists, gardeners, cooks and consumers have to come together to connect our history, tradition and the knowledge of food and seasonality that has been handed down through generations, with the right kind of research and technology. Only then can we tackle all the challenges we have to face, from desertification and water security to the acidification of the seas, and all the health problems we have brought upon ourselves by shamelessly reducing food to a mere cheap commodity.

I believe that people are demanding individuality and flavour again, and plant breeders and supermarkets are responding to that. At East Malling Research station for example, scientists are now developing some extraordinary varieties of fruit and vegetables, especially strawberries that, yes, have shelf life, and yes, have resistance to disease, but also have wonderful, complex flavours.

I am only a tiny firefly briefly passing by – but I am proud to be a part of this amazing team that is building something that will go beyond me, inviting people to think, and involving and exciting children to see what is possible. We are the generation who ate everything without asking a single question, but I believe that our children will be the ones who will reconnect with the true nourishment of food and where it comes from, embrace sustainable values and harness science in a good way so that they can create their own food revolution.

It was such a joy for me to work with Kate Humble who co-presented the TV series – we share a love of growing, of food, and we have similar ideologies and a great respect for the history, botanical knowledge and research that we were privileged to be a part of at Kew. Of course we didn't take ourselves too seriously; we had a lot of fun with our amazing film crew from Lion TV, and I hope we told our big, big story in an entertaining way. Most of all I owe a huge debt to our wonderful gardeners: the serene Alice Lumb and inquisitive Joe Archer, who nurtured our lovely produce day by day. And my two angels: Anne-Marie Owens, who has been with me for 29 years; and the gentle Anna Greenland, who looks after the vegetable garden and carries old wisdom and a deep understanding of the seasons in her young soul, which is beautiful to see. What a team. Between them they have researched and sowed the seeds and nurtured them. Together we have reaped the harvest, and with Adam and Ben, my trusty lieutenants in the kitchen, I have created completely new recipes to celebrate the purity and nobility of fruit and vegetables.

No more can we sustain the impact on our environment of eating so much meat. Vegetables, especially, are going to find their proper place in our diet – and I have to thank my partner Natalia Traxel for all her nutritional expertise on that subject! Hopefully we will all recognise the power of fruits and vegetables to affect our well-being, above all when they are fresh from the earth – which means growing more produce locally or in our own gardens.

You are what you eat. The first time I heard that expression I was 19 and deciding I wanted to be a chef. I was reading everything I could about food and health and it seemed like a complete over-statement. But the more I discovered about food and nutrition, the more I totally agreed with it. From seed to plate we have grown, organically, a magnificent garden at Kew, which embraces British heritage, soil and local varietals. Maybe I am a foolish romantic, but I believe this project will go some way to show that food is not a mere commodity; it connects with every part of our lives, and I hope this book will inspire people with these exciting ideas. Why not sow some seeds tomorrow, water them and watch them grow, then cook something wonderful for your loved ones. Please, do it. Because if we begin to reconnect our food with the garden, with seasonality, community, cooking, nutrition, science and the environment, then maybe we can help change the world... just a little.

Raymond, Kate and gardeners Alice and Joe enjoy the fruits of their labours.

PREPARING THE GARDEN

AS LADY EVE BALFOUR, the first president of the Soil Association, famously pronounced, 'the health of soil, plant, animal and man is one and indivisible.' Everything in the garden begins with the soil, and that means careful preparation before you begin planting.

Most gardens will benefit from digging in some well-rotted manure or garden compost, either in the autumn before spring sowing or planting, or a few weeks in advance if you are putting in seeds or seedlings at other times of the year.

However, Anna, who is in charge of Raymond's vegetable gardens at Le Manoir and worked with the team at Kew to prepare the beds for planting, advises that the key is to tailor your plan for enriching the soil to what is possible, given the size of your garden, and the area where you live. 'You may have a lot of kitchen waste and a reasonable sized vegetable plot which will give you leafy and woody cuttings, in which case you should be able to get a good compost heap going', she says. 'Or, if you live in a village with stables just down the road, you might have a great supply of well-rotted manure, which you could mix with your compost (the best possible scenario) or use on its own. If you have space to fill empty beds with a green manure crop (see page 15) you can make good use of that as a manure on its own or in addition to the compost heap; or alternatively, if you are surrounded by trees, you can rot down the fallen autumn leaves to make a fantastic mulch. If you live in a city with a small garden, then just buy a good non-peat all-purpose compost. It might be that you use compost one year and well-rotted manure the next. The thing to remember is that any bare ground should be covered over winter, so put down some form of enrichment – whatever is easiest – that will be absorbed into the soil and will feed it.'

Composting
For a seasoned gardener a well-ripened compost heap is almost as exciting as growing fruits and vegetables. 'Soil is an incredible living entity,' says Alice, who with fellow gardener Joe has tended the fruit and vegetable garden at Kew from its inception. 'When you add organic matter to it, this is gradually broken down by micro-organisms, earthworms, beetles, ants, etc. Bacteria and fungi living in the soil then work on the organic compounds, making nutrients available for the plant roots to take up.

'An extra benefit of adding compost to a free-draining, light sandy soil such as ours at Kew, is that it works like a sponge, helping to hold moisture in the soil and slow down the leaching of nutrients through it,' she says. 'We incorporate compost into all the beds and sometimes also use a thin layer as a top dressing during the growing season. Provided the soil has been well prepared in this way that is all that is needed, although I also like to sprinkle some Soil Association-certified organic chicken manure pellets around the base of fruit trees and bushes and some young vegetables. They will get absorbed into the soil when it rains and provide a good slow-release fertiliser.

'Once we have harvested a crop, it is always good to bump up and feed the soil again with another helping of compost.'

Kew's own, massive compost heap is in an area of the Gardens called the Stable Yard. Here some 4–6,000 cubic metres of compost is produced every year from woody material and herbaceous cuttings from the gardens, which are shredded and then mixed with manure (predominantly hay) that is brought in each week from the Royal Horse Artillery Stables in Woolwich and watered with rain water, which is collected and filtered close by. The process of mixing in the water also incorporates oxygen from the air, which starts off the bacterial and fungal breakdown. The decomposing material heats up naturally to 60°C (the temperature is checked using a probe), which is hot enough to kill any weed seeds and disease organisms. The compost will be rotted down and ready to use in 8–10 weeks, needing only an occasional sprinkling of rain water along the way, plus turning – using a digger, as the heap is so big!

There are many opinions on what makes a good compost heap but essentially they fall into two categories: aerobic and anaerobic.

Aerobic composting, as practiced by the Kew gardeners, and also known as hot composting, produces the best weed- and disease-free compost. As its name suggests, the continual presence of air accelerates the decomposition. However you need a reasonable volume of waste to generate the high temperature required. You also need a balance of finely shredded or chopped woody, carbon-rich material and lush, leafy nitrogen-rich material. Roughly speaking, you need to work on two-thirds woody material to one-third leafy material. You will need to turn the heap fairly regularly to introduce more air, in order to keep the temperature up and the whole process going. And occasionally you may need to add water, 'but generally in the UK, especially in winter, the heap will have enough natural moisture; and if it gets too wet it could turn anaerobic, as water replaces oxygen,' advises Anna.

When the compost is ready, the original material will no longer be distinguishable, and the compost will be dark brown to black, crumbly and full of worms, with a rich, sweet earthy smell.

Anaerobic composting, on the other hand, requires little attention – you simply mound up your material in whatever ratio you like and leave it – however it is a slow process. It can take up to a year in a temperate climate, such as that of the UK, to mature and the end product won't be as good.

What to use in your compost heap:
- Almost any material of vegetable origin: peelings, citrus peel (in moderation), egg shells, tea leaves, tea bags.
- Green garden waste, woody prunings (shredded or chopped into small pieces, which will break down quickly), lawn mowings and rotted straw.
- Animal and bird manures.
- Shredded paper, soaked in water, can also be added.

What to avoid:
- Any diseased crops, such as those affected by onion white rot (see page 117), clubroot (see page 262) or blight (see page 27).
- Perennial weeds, especially bindweed or ground elder.
- Scraps of meat, which pose a health risk as they attract vermin.
- Anything that doesn't rot, such as plastic or man-made fibres.

Digging

The purpose of digging a bed is to aerate the soil and so encourage good bacterial activity. By breaking up compacted clumps of soil you will also allow roots to penetrate more deeply, and at the same time expose weed seeds which can be picked out, as well as insect pests which will be exposed to the birds.

Deep, heavy digging is best done with a spade, using a fork for lighter work towards the surface.

Heavy clay soils are best dug in autumn or early winter in dry weather. If you leave it until spring, when the soil tends to be wetter, you risk damaging the structure. Conversely, light, sandy soils, such as that at Kew, shouldn't be dug in dry spells, as too much moisture will be lost.

No dig

Having said all this, some organic gardeners prefer not to dig at all in order to save the soil structure from disruption and potential damage. Instead, mulches of compost or well-rotted manure are used, which retain moisture, suppress weeds, add fertility and encourage an active earthworm population which will distribute the compost and manures. 'Crops grow well in this system,' says Anna, 'and you will save both time and your back!'

Mulching

A mulch is any material laid on the surface of the soil, such as straw, woodchips, compost, black matting or plastic, which can help protect the soil. While a plastic mulch is the most effective in terms of eliminating perennial weeds, the best mulches are organic matter, which will eventually break down into the soil and add fertility. Keeping the soil covered generally increases its productivity, helps keeps it cool in summer and warm in winter and traps in the moisture, which is useful in areas where there is low rainfall. It also protects the soil from compacting when walked on.

Green manure

These are specific crops that are grown on a spare piece of ground expressly to dig back into the top 15cm or so of soil in order to improve its structure and increase its levels of organic matter, nitrogen and general nutrient levels. Usually the plants are cut and allowed to wilt on the surface of the soil, before being incorporated. They can also be used on the compost heap, or as a mulch (see above). Allow 2–3 weeks in warm weather (around

four in cold weather and up to six if your crop includes clover and/or grazing rye), between incorporating a green manure and sowing your next crops, otherwise it can inhibit their growth.

There are three main categories of green manure crops:

- Fast-growing, leafy plants, such as mustard, fodder radish and phacelia, which help prevent the leaching of nutrients and suppress weeks.

- Leguminous plants such as peas, beans, clover and alfafa, which have nodules on their roots that also fix nitrogen in the soil. When the plants are harvested the nitrogen left behind will release slowly.

- Fibrous, dense-rooted crops such as grazing rye (one of the best for preventing the leaching of nutrients) improve the soil's structure as the roots push through it, and when dug in, they help to increase organic matter.

Leaf compost

Don't waste autumn leaves as they will eventually decay into wonderful leaf 'mould' for mulching or adding to compost. However be aware that the leaves may take up to two years to rot down completely, though you can speed this up by keeping the pile moist, and turning it regularly as you would do with compost.

Top: Kate and Raymond reap an early harvest of potatoes, and above: the fruit and vegetable garden at Kew is as aesthetically beautiful as it is bountiful.

COOK'S NOTES

My 'emulsion' method for vegetables

My favourite way to celebrate vegetables as an accompaniment to meat or fish is to cook them using my 'emulsion' method, a simple but stunning technique that seals in as much taste, texture, colour and goodness as possible.

For me the worst form of aggression is to boil a vegetable (except for asparagus, see page 75) because you are washing away flavour. And when the vegetable contains vitamin C, which is soluble in water, you lose the vitamin when you drain your vegetable. I want to increase flavour and keep in as many of the nutrients as possible. So I just put the vegetable – freshly podded peas, broad beans, finely sliced carrots, leeks, cabbage, turnips or young spinach – in a pan with just a few tablespoons of water, a knob of butter, a small pinch of sea salt and some black pepper. You can add a little crushed garlic – it is up to you.

I put the lid on my pan so it is sealed tightly, and then if I am roasting a piece of meat or fish I will have the pan sitting on the hob all ready to go (with no heat!) At the last minute I will turn on the heat to full, so the vegetables cook very fast: for around a minute for spinach; 3–4 for peas; 4–5 for leeks and carrots; and around 5 for beans. Turnips will take about 7 minutes (and you may need a little more water); it depends on how thinly you have cut your vegetables. The moment the vegetables are tender take the pan off the heat and if you like finish with some chopped herbs, maybe tarragon or parsley.

The butter and water will have mixed with a little escaping vegetable juice to create a lovely, light delicate emulsion, which lubricates and enfolds the vegetables. They will taste beautiful – and no draining away of vitamins! *Voilà!* Serve your vegetables with your roasted fish or meat, a glass of Pinot Noir or Chablis... life is perfect.

I only use organic fruits and vegetables as well as organic or free-range eggs.

Vegetables are medium-sized unless otherwise stated. Make sure you wash them before use; take extra care with salad leaves.

Onions and garlic are peeled unless otherwise indicated.

Herbs are fresh unless otherwise stated.

When using the zest of citrus fruit, buy organic or unwaxed.

Use good-quality sea salt – not refined table salt that usually contains anti-caking additives.

In some recipes the temperature is important, so you will need to use a kitchen thermometer/probe.

When sterilising jars for jams, put the jars into a large pan, cover completely with water, bring to the boil and then continue to boil on a high heat for 10 minutes. Lift out with tongs and allow to drip dry upside down on a clean wire rack. Fill while both the jars and the jam are still hot.

POTATOES

'I LOVE THE IDEA of a vegetable as humble as the potato being at the heart of some of the world's greatest dishes. What a huge and important gastronomic history it has,' says Raymond Blanc. 'I have spent most of my life cooking and growing many different varieties of potato. We harvest them and then run blind trials in my restaurant kitchen, giving marks for the taste, textures and performance when each one is roasted, puréed and fried, to try to find the ultimate potato for each technique. I am still as curious as a child to discover different, exciting varieties.'

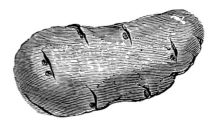

It is difficult to imagine a world without potatoes, but when they were first seen in Europe they were largely shunned as suspicious, possibly even poisonous.

Given the British love of potatoes it is hard to imagine a world without them and amusing to think that when the first specimens reached the British Isles from the Americas in the 1550s, they were viewed as strange, suspicious and, being a member of the nightshade family, probably poisonous. Little did the doubters know that in the twenty-first century potatoes would become the fifth most important food crop in the world (after rice, wheat, soy beans and maize).

Originally grown in the Andes between 7,000 and 10,000 years ago, it was in Peru, most likely around Lake Titicaca, that the Incas first developed the farming of potatoes on a sophisticated scale, building a system of terrace and irrigation systems and fertilising the earth with anchovies, which they knew to be rich in nutrients. In the hope of a bountiful harvest they worshipped the goddess of potatoes, Axomama, daughter of the earth mother Pachamama. In Peru and Bolivia the locals even developed one of the earliest forms of preservation, harnessing the local climate to create 'chuño' – dehydrated potato. The potatoes were left on the ground over the freezing nights then exposed to the hot sun during the day. During the process they were regularly stomped on in bare feet to press out all the moisture.

It was the Spanish conquistadors, having sailed to Peru in search of a different treasure – gold – who brought the potato back to Europe, where these novel tubers were greeted with none of the reverence afforded to them in the Andes. Sailors may have accepted them as a staple food for long voyages, but amongst the wider population they were shunned. It wasn't until the eighteenth century that they first began to find favour amongst the aristocracy. In Europe this was largely thanks to the efforts of Antoine Augustin Parmentier. A French agriculturalist and apothecary, he was captured while serving in the army during the Seven Years' War and while in prison in Prussia survived largely on potatoes, which the local peasants were forced to grow by royal decree. When he returned to his scientific work after the war, he was determined to publicise the nutritional merits of

Above (left and right): Second early Charlotte potatoes have the right waxy texture for spring salads, and (left), the delicate beauty of potato flowers once enticed Marie Antoinette to wear them in her hair.

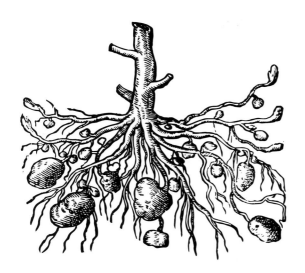

The Irish potato famine of 1845 was a salutory lesson to the world of the dangers of breeding out genetic diversity.

the potato amongst the French public, who still viewed it with suspicion. Realising he needed the endorsement of glamorous society, he began hosting elaborate dinners for celebrity guests at which potato dishes were served. As the story goes, he wooed the royal court by presenting King Louis XVI and his wife, Marie Antoinette, with white flowers from the potato plant, which the king wore in his buttonhole, and the queen entwined in her hair. The potato had acquired fashion status.

Poorer Europeans took longer to shed their mistrust, but steadily, through a combination of royal and governmental campaigns and the necessities forced by poverty and wars, potatoes at last began to be valued as a valuable source of nutrition, providing not only complex carbohydrate, but protein, vitamin C and calcium. As part of the Second World War effort, acres of potatoes were planted at Kew and tended by corps of women gardeners drafted in to demonstrate and teach people how to grow potatoes to help sustain their families in times of rationing.

Ironically, however, it was the over-dependence on the potato, more crucially a single variety, that led to the tragedy of the Irish famine back in 1845 when blight wiped out the entire potato crop. Smallholders had come to rely on tiny plots of land planted with potatoes to feed their families, but in one of the earliest examples of mono-cropping, had almost universally chosen one strain because it was higher yielding than others. When blight struck, ravaging 40 per cent of the crop, the tubers were left to rot in the fields, infecting the following year's crop, which then failed completely. Over a million people died, and around another 1–1.5 million were forced to leave Ireland, many of them packed aboard ships bound for America. Had a wider diversity of crops been planted, with different resistances to disease, the story may have been very different. It is a sobering reminder of the dangers of breeding out genetic diversity (a plant's natural ability to adapt to changing environments and threats from pests and disease) in the pursuit of growing homogenous, high-yielding crops. And as the task of feeding the world becomes more and more challenging in the face of changing global conditions, scientists in seed banks and research centres all over the world, notably Peru, are looking to the past to find answers for the future.

Charles Darwin wrote in wonder of the remarkable wild potatoes he discovered on his voyage to Chile.

Blight continues to be one of the few plant diseases that can completely destroy a crop. A single potato specimen collected during the height of the Irish famine and hidden away in Kew's cathedral-like Herbarium was recently analysed to provide new information on how the blight first appeared and then spread. At the Herbarium samples of plants dating back centuries are carefully preserved and annotated then kept in drawers that stretch from floor to ceiling. Some even include the handwritten notes of pioneering biologists like Charles Darwin, who wrote in his journal of the wonder of the wild potato he found on his five-year trip around the world collecting specimens. On the Chonos Archipelago, off the coast of Chile, he noted that it was 'remarkable that the same plant should be found on the sterile mountains of central Chile, where a drop of rain does not fall for more than six months, as well as within the damp forests of these southern islands.'

Of course diversity is not only the key to food security, but to individualism and flavour. Respect for variety is something Raymond has always known, having grown up helping dig and harvest the produce of his parents' garden in the Franche-Comté region of France. 'I always knew what my mum would be cooking by the variety she wanted from the garden. "Raymond, fetch me some Bintje," meant that we would be having fluffy purée made with butter and milk, or perhaps fish croquettes. "Raymond, some Maris Piper," told me it would be *pommes frites*, "Raymond, some Ratte," and it would be *rissolées* – potatoes that are blanched and then browned in butter and oil.'

'The maincrop potatoes (see page 26) would be stored in the cool of the cellar, which was really a giant *garde-manger* (larder), with its beaten earth floor which occupied the whole length of the house, and its diffused light which gave it an air of mystery. I loved to go in there after the harvest amongst the wooden crates of potatoes, beetroot, carrots and parsnips covered in jute sacks, and lined up on the shelves above, hundreds of jars and bottles of things pickled and preserved. The scents were magnificent, a mingling of earthiness, smokiness and wine, because there would be some smoked sausage or ham in the old-fashioned meshed meat safe, and my father also kept his wine in there in barrels from the local *vigneron* (wine-grower) so some drops would have fallen into the ground.'

In the garden at Kew, Alice and Joe have planted and nurtured 14 varieties of potato, chosen by Raymond. They include the classic French salad potato, Belle de Fontenay – 'a favourite in every French bistrot' – and the rather unromantically named International Kidney, which is the Jersey Royal, but as the famous potato now enjoys EU Protected Designation of Origin (PDO) status, only those potatoes grown on Jersey can bear the

Above: There is something very special and satisfying about pushing your fingertips into the earth and discovering a wonderful trove of potato treasure.

name. 'This respect for terroir is important,' applauds Raymond. 'The potatoes we can grow at Kew are equally beautiful, but of course the soil is different. On Jersey their garden is the sea, so traditionally the farmers used the seaweed washed up on the shores – they call it *vraic* – as a natural fertiliser to provide nitrogen, phosphorous, potassium and trace elements.

'For me Jersey Royals will always be the best of the earlies (see page 26) – something precious and delicate in flavour that we wait for and look forward to every spring, like the first peas or asparagus. You can do so many things with them, but I will always love them served with butter and a little sea salt, nothing else.'

Other heritage varieties being grown at Kew include the pale yellow-fleshed Bintje (early maincrop) that Raymond grew up with, and the Red Duke of York (first early) with its vivid coloured skin, which proved to be 'a revelation – a *coup de coeur* –I fell in love with this dream potato. It is very unusual for a potato to score so highly in our trials for roasting and chips *and* be good for puréeing too.' It is the experimental growing of the Agata (first early) variety however, that has really captured his enthusiasm, since, he says, this potato was responsible for 'my greatest ever potato experience two years ago'.

'I had taken my 92-year-old mother and my sister to the south of France for a little treat at a spa by the sea, and for lunch we went to a restaurant about 15 minutes away which you had to reach by boat – when we got there we discovered it was in the middle of a nudist colony. My mum didn't seem to mind the view though, so we sat down to a lunch of bouillabaisse, which was just divine. Beautiful fish, aïoli and the potatoes – I had never tasted anything like them: melting in texture, with a tinge of yellow in their flesh and a rich flavour that even alongside garlic and saffron still tasted of pure potato. Of course I had to know immediately what variety of potato this was. You can imagine how people thought I was crazy: on holiday in the sunshine in the middle of a nudist camp and getting excited about a potato! Eventually I found out from the boss of the restaurant that the variety was Agata. So it is my dream to be able to grow the Agata in a way that will match that memory.'

GROWING NOTES

Potatoes are grouped according to the season they are lifted – the idea being to keep a succession of varieties going all year round.

'Earlies' include new potatoes and other small varieties that are bred to grow fast and so will be ready to be pulled up in spring through to summer. They are quite fine-skinned and don't keep. They are at their absolute best when eaten on the same day as they are harvested, before their sugars turn to starch.

'Maincrop' varieties, on the other hand, can be left in the ground through the autumn until needed, then lifted and stored in sacks somewhere cool and dark over winter. They are larger, more robust and thicker-skinned.

Potatoes are not grown from seed, but from a potato from the previous year's crop, known as a seed potato. Since any disease will carry over into the next year's crop, it is best to buy commercially-grown seed potatoes, which are grown in sterile soil and certified disease-free.

Seed potatoes benefit from 'chitting' – the process of encouraging them to sprout before they are planted. 'It gives them a head start and encourages strong shoots to get going,' says Joe. 'It is very easy to do. Just look at your potatoes and you will see the 'eyes', the growing points from which the sprouts will form. Choose an area with four or five of these knobbly bits, scrub away any others and put the potatoes into empty egg boxes or seed trays, with the 'eyes' facing upwards. Leave the boxes or trays somewhere with some light and warmth, but not in direct sunlight until the shoots are about 2.5cm long. Chitting needs to be carried out a few weeks before planting, in late January/February, depending on the variety.'

When planting, choose a frost-free open site, which is not wet as excess moisture early in the season can produce leaf growth at the expense of the tubers. In the autumn before planting, dig in some well-rotted manure or compost.

Dig a trench around 8–15cm deep.

Plant the seed potatoes with the sprouting side upwards, 30–40cm apart (see opposite). The 'first early' varieties, which include new potatoes, should go in around the end of February to late March, 'second earlies', such as Belle de Fontenay, Maris Piper and Yukon Gold, around March to late May, and maincrop varieties from March to mid-May.

The 'first early' varieties will be quite small and ready 100–110 days from planting – around May or June, depending on the variety, and the 'second earlies', which are a little bigger (about the size of a hen's egg), will be ready in 110–120 days – around July.

Maincrop varieties should be ready within 125–140 days, depending on the weather conditions, i.e. they will be ready from around mid-July until early October.

Once the plants reach about 20cm in height, they start to develop the tubers at ground level, which will grow into the potatoes. It is very important the tubers are never exposed to any light as this turns them green, an indication of poisonous glycoalkaloids and the reason green potatoes should never be eaten. One way of

excluding the light is to grow the plants through black polythene, however the Kew gardeners favour 'earthing up' or 'banking', which involves piling up the earth around the stems of the plants, to keep the tubers in the dark. 'There may even be an added bonus in this method,' believes Alice, 'as the more earth you heap around the stem, the more this encourages roots to develop and in turn this means plants put out more tubers, so you may increase your yield.'

Be vigilant in watching for blight.
'Unfortunately it is difficult to pre-empt,' says Alice, 'you just have to be watchful, and the moment you spot any brown patches or lesions on the stems or see the leaves beginning to curl, take the tops off the plants to reduce the spread, otherwise the wind and rain will carry the spores into the ground and into the tubers. Certain combinations of temperature and rainfall, known as Smith Periods, are conducive to the spread of blight. You can register with the Potato Council to receive alerts about them.'

If blight does take hold, clear and burn any infected foliage and avoid adding any to compost as spores can overwinter on the heap. Remove all infected tubers from the soil and burn these too.

Around the allotted harvest time you can start digging your potatoes. Even if you have lost track of when exactly you planted each variety, a good indication is when the flowers are open in the case of maincrops. However this is just a guide. If you like your potatoes smaller, there is nothing to stop you digging them up a little earlier. Do a test first by pulling away the soil around the plant with your fingers until you unearth a potato and can see that it is the size you want. Then use a fork (preferably flat pronged), rather than a spade, so you don't accidentally slice through a potato. Go in at an angle, a little distance away from the plant and lift up the soil to reveal the rest of the treasures!

RAYMOND'S FLAVOUR NOTES

Although certain varieties are better suited to particular cooking methods, some are brilliant all-rounders (see page 36). It is worth remembering that the longer a maincrop potato is stored, the more it loses moisture and develops its starch levels (up to the point that it begins to sprout), so a newly harvested potato will behave slightly differently to one that has been kept for three months. If you sauté an older potato, for example, the higher starch and sugar levels will cause it to brown more quickly; and if you purée it, the result might be slightly sticky.

For roasting, Yukon Gold (second early) and Red Duke of York (first early) are my favourites. I had rarely had a good roast potato in France, because the French roast them from raw, so I discovered the technique for great roast potatoes in England. Now I think, very immodestly, of course, they are one of my best achievements – though I have to acknowledge that it was Adam, my right hand man for 11 years, who first showed me how to 'ruffle' potatoes, and now I ruffle every Sunday! I cook the potatoes gently, with just five, six, seven bubbles breaking the surface, so that I keep in the flavour and nutrients, but also steam away the outer layer of starch to let moisture in, which keeps them moist in the oven and stop them 'shrinkling' – my word for shrinking and crinkling! Ruffle them in a colander so that the edges will crisp up beautifully when you roast them to a golden blonde in hot duck fat. Personally I think duck fat is the best for flavour and health because it contains mono-unsaturated fats, which carry some extraordinary antioxidants. It is part of the south-west France paradox that people live until they are 110 years old but eat lots of foie gras and duck fat and drink red wine. You could use rapeseed oil, too, which is also good from a nutritional point of view (it is high in omega oils 3, 6 and 9; lower in saturated fats than other oils; and a source of vitamin E). Also, it has a higher 'smoke point', which allows it to be heated to a high temperature without losing its character and nutritional values. And many cooks use beef fat.

For chips and for sautéing, again I would choose Red Duke of York or Yukon Gold and maincrop Agria. If you sauté potatoes from raw, their starches and sugars can cause them to brown before they are cooked through, so I blanch the potatoes briefly first, just for about a minute, as this takes out some of the starch. Then I drain them and let them steam in a colander until completely dry, so they will crisp up well. I like to start them in vegetable oil, then add some butter to the pan, and at the last minute finish them, as my mother used to do, with *persillade*, the wonderful mixture of chopped shallots, garlic and parsley known in every French household.

Pommes soufflées will always be a miracle of chemistry for me. It is dazzling that you can blanch a slice of potato in oil, then fry it a second time in hotter oil and it will puff up into the perfect flying saucer shape. For this I think Maris Piper is the best variety.

For *purée*, Estima (second early) is excellent, as well as Belle de Fontenay (second early), Rocket (first early), and maincrop Agria, as they have the right texture.

For steaming and for salads, I would choose waxier potatoes that will hold together, such as my favourite – Jersey Royals (first early), as well as Belle de Fontenay or Charlotte (second early).

Right: Solanum tuberosum *from* Vervolg op de Afbeeldingen der artseny-gewassen met derzelver Nederduitsche en Latynsche beschryvingen, *vol. 1: t.45 (1813) by German botanist and pharmacist Johannes Zorn, translated into Dutch by botanist Dirk Leonard Oskamp.*

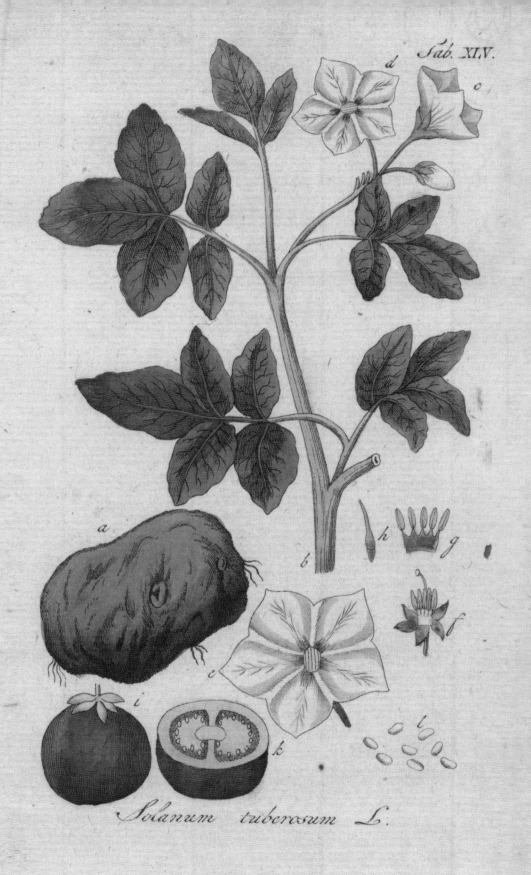

Tab. XLV.

Solanum tuberosum L.

NEW POTATO AND CHORIZO TORTILLA

Many countries have their own version of an open omelette. The Italians have frittata, the Spanish tortilla. In France it is Spanish omelette. Traditionally it wouldn't be new season potatoes used in this dish – it would be bigger maincrop potatoes – but I wanted to celebrate the first of the early potatoes and they worked surprisingly well. As the season goes on, you could substitute Belle de Fontenay and other different varieties, such as Agria: you just don't want a potato that is too floury as it will break up.

SERVES 4–6

Preparation time: 10 minutes
Cooking time: 35 minutes

400g Jersey Royal potatoes, quartered
1 onion, diced
1 garlic clove, finely chopped
3 tbsp olive oil
2 bay leaves
1 thyme sprig
1 rosemary sprig
pinch Espelette pepper or smoked paprika
pinch sea salt
120g chorizo, cut into small dice
15g flat-leaf parsley, finely chopped
80g spinach, chopped
8 eggs, whisked

Preheat the oven to 170°C/Gas Mark 3½.

In a medium sauté pan with a lid, over a medium heat, sweat the potatoes, onion and garlic in the oil with the bay leaf, thyme, rosemary, Espelette pepper or smoked paprika and salt for 13–15 minutes. Stir regularly to avoid any colouring.

Add the chorizo and continue to sweat for 5 minutes with the lid on so the flavours mingle. Finally, add the parsley and spinach and stir them into the vegetables for 30 seconds, then remove from the heat, add the eggs and stir everything together until evenly mixed.

Pour the egg mixture into a 20cm non-stick ovenproof frying pan and place in the oven for 15 minutes. Once cooked, remove from the oven and leave to rest for 5 minutes before turning out on to a board or a large serving dish. Using a serrated knife, cut the omelette into 4–6 wedge-shaped slices and serve warm.

Variation
This dish offers hundreds of opportunities for interpretation using different vegetables and herbs – be as creative as you like.

SAUTE POTATOES WITH PERSILLADE AND LARDONS

Many of us celebrate the arrival of new potatoes in the humblest manner – simply boiled and tossed with a knob of butter, and it is one of the greatest ways to eat them. But I also find that new potatoes pan-fry extremely well. Of course, as the seasons change you can move on to different varieties of potato. As a Frenchman I must throw in a classic persillade at the last minute. At its heart this is garlic, shallots and parsley, to which you can add other herbs if you like – I suggest chervil and tarragon.

SERVES 4

Preparation time: 5 minutes
Cooking time: 10 minutes

For the potatoes
300g Jersey Royal or other new
    potatoes, halved
600ml water

For the persillade
30g flat-leaf parsley, chopped
5g chervil, chopped
4 tarragon leaves, chopped
½ banana shallot, finely chopped
1 garlic clove, puréed

To finish
2 tbsp rapeseed oil
100g smoked bacon lardons
20g unsalted butter
pinch sea salt
2 pinches freshly ground black
    pepper

For the potatoes, in a large saucepan on a high heat, simmer the potatoes in the water for 5 minutes, then drain in a colander and leave to stand for 1 minute so the steam can escape. Reserve.

For the persillade, simply mix the ingredients in a small bowl.

To finish, in a large frying pan over a high heat, heat the oil and colour the bacon lardons, then add the cooked potatoes, then the butter. Season with the salt and black pepper and cook for 10 minutes, stirring every minute, until golden brown. Spoon out any fat from the pan and stir in the persillade. Taste and adjust the seasoning if necessary. Serve immediately.

Chef's note
Although you can sauté the potatoes from raw, I prefer to blanch them first as they have a high starch content, which will convert into sugar and cause them to brown too fast. By blanching them you are neutralising the starches, which will give the potato a better texture and colour.

SEA TROUT, NEW POTATOES AND WATERCRESS SAUCE

English watercress is wonderfully tasty, peppery and nutritious – full of vitamins C and E and ß-carotene, which is converted into vitamin A in the body, as well as calcium. The sauce makes more than you need but this is the minimum quantity that can be blended. It can be frozen for up to four weeks.

SERVES 4

Preparation time: 5 minutes
Cooking time: 20 minutes

For the sea trout
4 sea trout fillets (about 120g
    each), skin on
20g unsalted butter
2 tbsp water
juice of ¼ lemon

For the potatoes
300g new potatoes, halved
600ml water
1½ tsp sea salt

For the watercress sauce
250g watercress leaves
70ml extra virgin olive oil
50ml water
sea salt and freshly ground black
    pepper

To serve
watercress leaves

For the watercress sauce, blanch the watercress in boiling water for 30 seconds to remove some of the bitterness, then refresh in iced water. Place in a large colander and squeeze out as much water as possible. Chop and transfer to a blender with the olive oil, water and a pinch of salt and pepper. Blend on full speed, then taste and correct the seasoning if necessary. Pass through a fine sieve and warm in a pan when ready to serve.

For the potatoes, in a large saucepan on a medium heat, bring the potatoes, water and salt to a boil. Turn down the heat and cook for 12 minutes on a gentle simmer then turn off the heat and leave in the cooking liquor until the trout is ready.

For the trout fillets, first pat the fish dry with kitchen paper. Season lightly with salt and pepper. In a large non-stick frying pan on a medium heat, cook the butter until it starts to turn a nutty hazelnut brown. Place the trout in the pan, skin-side down. Very fresh fish will arc upwards at this point so, using a fish slice press the fillets down for a few seconds so they keep contact with the pan and stay flat.

Cook the trout fillets for 7–8 minutes depending on their thickness, until the skin is crisp. You should hear just a gentle sizzle as the skin browns and crisps beautifully and there should be no smoke rising from the pan. Too much heat will overcook the fish and the butter will burn.

Turn the fillets over on to the flesh side and cook for a further minute. Remove the trout from the pan and leave to rest for 1 minute on a warm plate. Stir the water and lemon juice into the pan juices.

To serve, place a small pile of the cooked potatoes in the centre of each plate, brush the sea trout with the pan juices and place on top of the potatoes. Drizzle the warmed sauce around the plate and finish by scattering over a few watercress leaves.

A POTATO IN THE KITCHEN

Raymond's favourites for...

★ Best for | ✥ Best all-rounders

ROAST

Yukon Gold ★
(second early)

Red Duke of York ✥ ★
(first early)

Rocket
(first early)

Belle de Fontenay
(second early)

Agria
(maincrop)

Desiree ✥
(maincrop)

Pink Fir Apple ✥
(maincrop)

Maris Piper
(maincrop)

CHIPS AND SAUTE

Red Duke of York ✥ ★
(first early)

Yukon Gold
(second early)

Agria
(maincrop)

Rocket
(first early)

Desiree ✥
(maincrop)

Pink Fir Apple ✥
(maincrop)

Maris Piper
(maincrop)

MASH AND PUREE

Estima ★
(second early)

Belle de Fontenay ★
(second early)

Rocket
(first early)

Agria
(maincrop)

Red Duke of York ✥
(first early)

Desiree ✥
(maincrop)

Pink Fir Apple ✥
(maincrop)

SALADS

Jersey Royals ★
(first early)

Belle de Fontenay
(second early)

Charlotte
(second early)

Pink Fir Apple ✥
(maincrop)

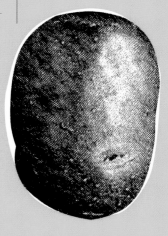

RHUBARB

RHUBARB

WEARS TWO different faces: tender, sophisticated, startlingly pink and grown in darkness; or sturdy, assertive and reassuringly homely, flourishing in the open air. Each has its season, each has its champions.

It wasn't until the eighteenth century that rhubarb first began to be valued for its stalks rather than its roots, which had previously been powdered for medicinal purposes.

We think of rhubarb as quintessentially English, appearing as it does in a wealth of traditional puddings, but not only is it classed in Britain as a vegetable, rather than a fruit, it originally hails from China and Siberia, where it wasn't valued for culinary use, but as a drug. The roots were powdered and used for various medicinal purposes, typically as a purgative and laxative. At one time rhubarb was so prized that it was more expensive than saffron or opium, and botanists and apothecaries competed to find and classify the most potent and authentic of the different strains emanating from China or Russia, in the hope that they could ultimately identify the 'one true rhubarb'. In its medicinal form it arrived in Europe around the fifteenth century and was clearly known in England in Shakespearean times, since the Bard has his tragic hero Macbeth ask, as he takes the field before the battle at Dunsinane, 'What rhubarb, senna, or what purgative drug, Would scour these English hence?'

It wasn't until the seventeenth century, however, that Yorkshireman Sir Matthew Lister, physician to Charles I, introduced the growing of rhubarb to Britain – still for its roots, rather than its stalks, using seeds he had sourced from a botanic garden in Italy. By the second half of the eighteenth century, the first references to the rhubarb stalks being cooked and made into tarts began to appear in cookery books, such as Hannah Glasse's *The Compleat Confectioner*, though such ideas were still something of a curiosity. Susanne Groom, former curator at Historic Royal Palaces and an authority on the royal kitchens at Kew Palace, notes that 'tincture of rhubarb, presumably prescribed as a purgative, is recorded in the household accounts for George III in his last years as Prince of Wales at Kew Palace (1757–60). It is also recorded as being administered to him during his illness of 1788–89.'

Isaac Oldaker, gardener to the botanist Joseph Banks, the first 'director' of the Botanic Gardens at Kew, was one of those who sought to grow rhubarb for culinary use. But it wasn't until 1817 that its fortunes were dramatically changed by one of those brilliant mistakes with which the history of food is peppered. One day at London's Chelsea Physic Garden, a garden worker accidentally piled soil over one of the rhubarb plants while digging a trench. Weeks later it was discovered that, deprived of light,

Above and left: In the darkness, lit only by candlelight, the tender and vibrantly pink Yorkshire Forced Rhubarb is still produced in the time-honoured fashion. Visitors to the forcing sheds talk of an almost mystical experience.

Above: Rheum spiciforme – *a less familiar, some say purgative relative of garden rhubarb* (Rheum rhabarbarum) *as depicted in a nineteenth-century watercolour on paper by an unidentified Indian artist, from the collection 'Royle, Carey and Others'.*

the plant was unable to photosynthesise and so put its energy not into growing leaves, but into producing tiny, vibrantly pink shoots. When they were tasted, these shoots were sweeter and more tender than any rhubarb that had previously been grown exposed to the elements.

It was the start of a new fashion. Anyone could 'blanch' rhubarb in this way by covering the growing plants with a bucket or terracotta plant pot, or simply piling straw over the top. By the time Queen Victoria was crowned in 1837 rhubarb was replacing gooseberry as the tart-flavoured fruit of choice. New varieties were named after Victoria and Albert, and rhubarb pies, jellies, cakes and jams were all the rage. In 1845, Eliza Acton's *Modern Cookery for Private Families* included a recipe for curate's pudding made by layering rhubarb and sugar with 'part of a penny roll sliced thin', finished with breadcrumbs, more sugar, and clarified butter, and then put into a 'brisk oven'. And in 1861, when Isabella Beeton, that other great touchstone for the tastes of Victorian times, published her *Book of Household Management*, she included a recipe for rhubarb wine, as well as rhubarb and orange jam 'to resemble Scotch marmalade'.

While London and Yorkshire flourished as centres of growing, it was in the 'triangle' of Wakefield, Leeds and Bradford that a new technique of 'forcing' this early pink rhubarb was developed. The terms 'forcing' and 'blanching' tend to be used interchangeably by gardeners, however technically 'blanching' refers simply to excluding the light, whereas 'forcing' refers to the idea of growing an early crop using the plant's own stored energy, and soil and sunlight are not required. In terms of the Yorkshire method, 'forcing' the rhubarb involves lifting the plants from the ground and growing them in the pitch dark in special sheds. In the nineteenth century, this 'frost pocket' of northern England was uniquely placed to fuel the process, since the sheds could be heated by coal from the local pits and the soil was nitrogen-rich, partly thanks to the composting of 'shoddy', a waste product from the local woollen mills. In order to prepare the rhubarb for the process, it was first allowed to grow outside in the nutrient-rich fields for two years without trimming or harvesting, so the plants could concentrate on forming heavy root balls full of carbohydrates that would be converted into energy during a good frost. At this point the plants were lifted and moved into the dark sheds. Here in the warmth and under a fine spray of water they were tricked into thinking it was spring, so they used their energy to produce the famously pink shoots.

Family growers vied with each other to grow the best strains of rhubarb, and guarded their own production secrets, which were handed

In the post-war years, new exotic fruits such as melons and pineapples began to eclipse rhubarb in popularity, but today it is enjoying a renaissance in both restaurant and home kitchens.

down through the generations. At the height of production in the run up to Christmas and for the short season that followed, up to 200 tons of forced rhubarb would be transported to the London markets every weeknight aboard a special train from Ardsley station; it came to be known as the 'rhubarb express'. Although the train continued running into the early 1960s, production was difficult during the Second World War as fuel shortages made it hard to heat the sheds, and the Ministry of Food judged the process of leaving the roots in the fields for two years as wasteful, ordering the stalks to be harvested and sent for jam-making. Sugar rationing also meant that the sharpness of rhubarb couldn't easily be tempered for home cooking. Then, in the post-war years when sweeter, imported exotic fruits such as pineapples and melons started to appear in British shops, these began to eclipse the rhubarb in popularity and the forcing business went into decline, with many producers going bankrupt, selling up or turning their attentions to other crops.

In the last few decades, though, the electric-pink forced rhubarb has become famous all over again, thanks to the dedication and determination of the remaining 12 producers, led by Janet Oldroyd Hulme, whose family has been forcing rhubarb in Yorkshire for five generations. The growers have tapped into a renewed respect amongst chefs and home cooks for local and traditional foods and in 2010 were able to achieve Protected Designation of Origin (PDO) status for Yorkshire Forced Rhubarb granted by the European Commission's Protected Food Name scheme. PDO guarantees the production area, correct practice and quality.

The production process has scarcely changed, except that warm air has replaced coal as the means of heating the sheds, and thermometers in the soil allow the two-year-old rhubarb to be lifted from the ground when the optimum number of frost units can convert into glucose all the energy that the plant has built up. Inside the forcing sheds, everything is done by candlelight to maintain the essential darkness, lending a magical feel to the sheds.

'Forced rhubarb plants are shrouded in such an aura of mystery and romance, like fragile prima donnas that have to be handled so gently,' says Raymond. 'They say you can hear them pop as the moisture and warmth triggers the buds to stretch and start to shoot. I tried; I listened very carefully. I swear I have heard a carrot cry when I pulled it from the earth, but in the flickering candlelight I didn't hear the rhubarb sing; there was only silence.'

The simpler method of garden 'forcing' is something that Raymond and his team follow every year using a single heritage variety, Timperley Early. Originally grown by the Baldwin family in Timperley in Cheshire

Above: For Raymond the flavour of rustic, open-air fruit wins out over early 'forced' pink rhubarb.

in the 1920s, it is 'forced' for the early part of the season and then allowed to grow on in the sunlight. 'As the name suggests, this is the earliest variety, so we can get a jump on the season and it gives the kitchen something quite special at quite a barren time of year,' says Anna, who is in charge of the process. 'We cover the plants with beautiful big terracotta cloches around December and January – it's a fun thing to do – then we take off the cloches and let the plants photosynthesise and grow naturally until around June, when the stalks become a little too thick and woody for the kitchen. At the end of summer the rhubarb channels its energy back into the roots where it is stored over winter ready to shoot again. We just give it a good dose of manure over the cold months and it takes care of itself.'

'My chefs all love the early pink rhubarb,' says Raymond, 'and I understand that, of course, because it is very beautiful, colourful – sexy, and it connects with a British tradition. But for pure flavour, I have to say I still prefer the later, rustic, open-air rhubarb because it has much more tartness. Its sugars build up slowly, as it faces the light and the cold, and as it grows more fibrous I believe it creates a stronger, longer structure of flavour.'

'In my parents' garden we had a huge, huge rhubarb bush that grew from one crown and is still growing after nearly 60 years – it was quite magnificent, disproportionately big, really, because it was beside the compost heap which fed the soil. In the winter we just cut it down, and the re-growth was incredible. My mother complains that the rhubarb isn't doing as well now, and I say, "of course, *Maman*. There is no longer a big family to feed, so the compost heap is not as big. You will have to give it some more food if you want it to last another 60 years!" When I was growing up she used to make the rhubarb into summer tarts, and compotes, which we had with semolina, and it is that flavour of outdoor rhubarb that I will always love.'

Accordingly at Kew, Anna, Alice and Joe chose to experiment with a new outdoor variety, the boldly-named Thompson's Terrifically Tasty, which is one of the earliest varieties, and it impressed Raymond enough to want to add it to his kitchen garden in Oxfordshire. 'It has a big flush of good stalks, which are really, really lovely,' says Raymond. 'I cooked it in all the ways that I love to do with rhubarb: I puréed it, diced it and cooked it in its own juices and the flavour was excellent.'

GROWING NOTES

Rhubarb is an easy perennial crop, which likes fertile, free-draining soil and an open, preferably sunny site. At Kew the plants are grown in the herbaceous borders edging the main vegetable garden. 'It doesn't like to be moved, though, so pick your spot carefully,' says Alice.

The best way to grow it is from a crown, rather than seed. These are established plants which are already a year old and will produce a crop in the harvest season (April–June) after planting.

Dig in plenty of well-rotted manure or compost in advance.

Plant in mid-autumn to early spring. 'At Kew we "top dress" with a layer of our own compost (i.e. add it as a mulch to the surface of the soil), to both help retain moisture and suppress competitive weeds,' says Alice. 'But when you mulch, don't do it right up to the crown of the rhubarb, as that could cause it to rot.'

Remove flowers as they arrive to divert the plant's energies into the stems, rather than seed. For your first harvest only take a third to half of the stalks each time you pull them, and mulch again with manure or compost in the autumn. If you strip the plant of stalks completely it will take longer to recover for the following season.

There are no real pest problems. 'Occasionally,' says Alice, 'the odd slug or snail might do a bit of damage, but it is pretty minimal.'

In the next year you can harvest steadily for around three months, but finish by the end of July to give the plant time to build up energy reserves again for the next year's crop.

Every five or six years, lift and divide the crowns to maintain their vigour and keep them productive.

If you can't wait until April for your first rhubarb, you might like to try 'forcing' the plants. If you are going to do this, it is best to grow a few plants so that you can avoid blanching the same crown two years in a row, as this can weaken the plant. Ideally, just blanch one plant a year, then let it replenish the following year while you choose another one to blanch, and so on in rotation.

Wait until a crown is two years old before forcing it for the first time.

In January cover the crown with a layer of straw, and then put a large container over the top to exclude the light. You can buy special decorative clay pots for this, but an upturned bucket or dustbin works equally well.

The bright ruby-red/pink stems will usually be ready for harvesting eight weeks after covering, usually up to a month earlier than rhubarb which is grown in the open air and light.

RAYMOND'S FLAVOUR NOTES

Early 'forced' rhubarb is delicate in flavour and has more sweetness than late rhubarb, and, of course, it has a beautiful, radiant, ruby-red/pink colour when raw and cooked.

Late rhubarb has a robust, potent flavour with greater acidity, which for me is the 'true' taste of rhubarb. If you still want the bright colour (or to soften the acidity), you can cheat by adding a drop of grenadine (pomegranate syrup) to the rhubarb when it is cooked. In fact, this isn't cheating, it is being clever!

Whether I use early or late rhubarb in a dessert, I like to chop and macerate it for up to half an hour in some sugar first. By doing this you extract the juices and intensify the flavour.

Never eat rhubarb leaves as they contain a high concentration of oxalic acid. This acid is found in many foods in safe doses, such as the stalks of rhubarb, Swiss chard, spinach, beetroot and even tea and cocoa, but the percentage of oxalic acid in rhubarb leaves makes them poisonous.

ROAST PIGEON, RHUBARB CHUTNEY AND CHICORY

I love the multicultural nature of British food, and especially chutneys, which have their roots in Anglo-Indian cooking. This is a lovely fresh chutney and the sharpness of the rhubarb cuts through the richness of the pigeon. It is an expensive starter, but I think worth it as it is created with the most delicious poultry – the Anjou squab, which has a wonderfully rich flavour. This dish also showcases the sweet bitterness of the chicory, which is flash-fried just to warm it through.

SERVES 4

Preparation time: 15 minutes, plus
   macerating
Cooking time: 30 minutes

For the rhubarb chutney
400g English rhubarb, cut into
   2cm batons
40g caster sugar
10g root ginger, finely grated
½ white onion, diced
30ml aged balsamic vinegar
50ml water
sea salt and freshly ground black
   pepper

For the pigeon
2 Anjou squabs

For the sauce
1½ tbsp rapeseed oil
20g unsalted butter
20g banana shallot, finely sliced
2 black peppercorns, crushed
60g field mushrooms, finely sliced
100ml Madeira
3 tbsp white wine
200ml Brown Chicken Stock (see
   page 280)
2 tsp whipping cream
1 thyme sprig
½ 'new season' garlic clove, crushed

Make the chutney. In a large bowl, mix the rhubarb with the sugar and ginger and leave to macerate for 15 minutes.

In a medium saucepan on a medium heat, cook the onion in the vinegar and water with a pinch of salt and pepper for 10 minutes, until the liquid has mostly reduced and evaporated. Add the macerated rhubarb, turn the heat up to high and cook for 4 minutes, until the rhubarb begins to break down and the juices are released. Remove from the heat and leave to cool.

To prepare the pigeons, chop the wings off close to the shoulder. Push the flesh surrounding the shoulder inwards. Remove the wishbone, cut off the neck and chop off the tailbone. Set aside the prepared pigeons and chop all the bones into small pieces to use in the sauce.

For the sauce, in a medium sauté pan on a high heat, lightly colour the pigeon bones in the rapeseed oil for 2 minutes. Reduce the heat, add the butter and cook until it starts to turn a hazelnut brown colour. Gently brown the bones in the nutty butter for a further 5 minutes. Add the sliced shallots, a pinch of salt and the crushed pepper and slowly brown for 5 minutes, until light golden. Add the mushrooms and sweat for a further 5 minutes.

In a small saucepan, boil the Madeira for 30 seconds, then add the white wine and boil for a further 30 seconds. Add to the shallot mixture to deglaze the pan, scraping any browned bits from the bottom with a wooden spoon. Add the chicken stock, cream, thyme and garlic. Bring to the boil, skimming off any fats and impurities that rise, and simmer for 10 minutes. Pass through a sieve into a small pan. Taste, adjust the seasoning and reserve.

Continued overleaf $\rightarrow$

To cook the pigeons
30g unsalted butter

To finish the sauce
30g unsalted butter
dash of sherry vinegar
1 tsp aged dry Madeira

To serve
1 red chicory, leaves separated
1 yellow chicory, leaves separated
½ head frisée

Preheat the oven to 100°C/Gas Mark ¼.

To cook the pigeons, first season the squabs lightly with salt. In a small ovenproof frying pan over a medium heat, melt the butter until it starts to turn a nutty hazelnut brown colour. Brown the pigeons on their side in the butter for 3 minutes on each side. Cook with the breast face down for a further 3 minutes.

Place the squabs in the oven for 8 minutes. Probe the centre of the breasts to ensure there is a core temperature of 60°C, then remove from the oven. Using a sharp knife, carve off the legs and breasts. Roll the pigeon breast and legs in the roasting juices in the pan.

Set aside on a small tray in a warm place (a low oven or the back of your hob), loosely covered with tin foil. Chop the cooked carcass into 3cm pieces with meat secateurs.

To finish the sauce, in a medium saucepan on a medium heat, melt the butter until it starts to turn a nutty hazelnut brown colour, add the chopped carcass pieces and brown for 5 minutes.

Spoon the butter out of the pan and discard, add the pigeon sauce and simmer for 5 minutes. Skim off any impurities and taste. Add the sherry vinegar and the Madeira. Taste again and correct the seasoning. If it lacks sharpness, add a hint more sherry vinegar. Strain the sauce into a small saucepan and reserve. You will have about 150ml of sauce.

To serve, place a spoonful of the chutney down the centre of each plate and layer the carved pigeon on top. Arrange the chicory and salad leaves around each dish and finish by drizzling the sauce around.

RHUBARB AND CUSTARD

This dessert is a celebration of a quintessentially British fruit. What excites the tastebuds as much as different flavours is contrasting textures, so in this dessert we have tart rhubarb jelly studded with tender fruit; sweet, smooth, velvety, custard; and a garnish of crisp dried rhubarb.

SERVES 4

Preparation time: 1 hour
Cooking time: 1 hour

For the dried rhubarb crisp
1 rhubarb stick
100ml water
20g caster sugar
10ml grenadine syrup

For macerating and cooking the rhubarb (yields 360g rhubarb and 200ml juice)
450g rhubarb, cut into 1cm pieces
45g caster sugar

Continued overleaf $\longrightarrow$

Place 4 glasses or glass serving dishes in the fridge to chill thoroughly. Preheat the oven to 100°C/Gas Mark ¼.

For the dried rhubarb crisp, with a sharp vegetable peeler, carefully shave the rhubarb lengthways until you have at least six nice pieces and place these in a small bowl. Chop the remaining rhubarb into 1cm pieces and reserve this for when you make the cooked rhubarb compote.

In a small saucepan on a high heat, bring the water, sugar and grenadine syrup to a gentle simmer, add the shaved rhubarb slices then turn off the heat and leave to cool for 10 minutes.

Drain the slices of rhubarb, reserving the syrup for macerating the rhubarb, and place on a baking tray lined with a silicone mat. Place in the oven for 25 minutes to dry out then store in an airtight container until needed. Increase the oven temperature to 140°C/Gas Mark 1.

To macerate the rhubarb, in a large bowl mix the rhubarb (including the reserved chopped rhubarb) and sugar with 100ml of the reserved rhubarb syrup and leave to macerate for 30 minutes. Transfer to a shallow oven tray and cover tightly with cling film to create a seal and ensure that none of the juice will evaporate. Place in the oven for 25 minutes.

Once cooked, transfer to the fridge to cool down in its own syrupy juice before straining this off and reserving it. Finely chop half of the cooked rhubarb (this will be about 180g), leaving the rest as it is and set aside in two separate mounds.

Measure 200ml of the reserved syrupy juice to make the jelly.

Continued overleaf $\longrightarrow$

For the jelly

2 thin slices root ginger

1½ gelatine leaves, softened in
    cold water and drained

For the custard (makes 475ml)

150ml whipping cream

150ml milk

100g caster sugar

2 tsp Vanilla Purée (see page 281)
    or good-quality vanilla extract

6 egg yolks

1 gelatine leaf, softened in cold
    water and drained

For the honeycomb

40ml water

35g clear honey

70g liquid glucose

200g caster sugar

20g bicarbonate of soda

For the jelly, in a small saucepan on a low heat, infuse the ginger in the 200ml of reserved cooking juice for 5 minutes along with the softened gelatine and stir to dissolve the gelatine. Strain, reserving 80ml for building the trifle and pour the remainder into a small bowl.

Start to build your trifle before you make the custard. Place 40g of the reserved finely chopped cooked rhubarb in the bottom of each chilled glass. Top with 50g of the larger reserved cooked rhubarb pieces. Pour 20ml of the reserved jelly liquid into each glass and place in the bottom of your fridge for 15 minutes, until the jelly has just set.

Make the custard. In a medium saucepan on a medium heat, bring the cream, milk, sugar and vanilla purée to a boil. In a large bowl, whisk the egg yolks.

Once the cream mixture comes to the boil, pour over the beaten egg yolks and whisk until evenly distributed. Pour this mixture back into the pan on a medium heat and bring it to 75ºC, making sure you stir all the time. Take off the heat and place the pan inside a bowl of iced water. Using a hand-held blender, blitz in the softened gelatine and continue to blend until the custard is cool. By whisking as it cools you will add a third more volume thanks to the lightness of the air that is being incorporated.

It is important that the custard sets in the glass you are going to serve it in otherwise the more you stir the set custard the more you will lose all the air bubbles and ultimately the lightness of the dessert. So, take each of the desserts from the fridge, top each one with custard and return to the fridge to set for 3 hours minimum and overnight if you have the time.

Meanwhile, prepare the honeycomb. Line a 20 x 25 x 3cm tray with a silicone mat. Put the water, then the honey, glucose and sugar into a medium saucepan and leave for a minute while the sugar dissolves. Place the pan on a high heat and bring to the boil. Reduce to a medium heat and cook for 5 minutes, until you have a light golden caramel.

Continued overleaf $\longrightarrow$

To serve (optional)

young angelica
    shoots, finely sliced

Take off the heat and stir in the bicarbonate of soda. There will be a huge amount of frothing and bubbling and it will increase in volume by about five times. This is caused by the bicarbonate of soda reacting with the heat of the sugar, which produces the bubbles that will eventually create a crunchy honeycomb. Beware – it is a very pretty spectacle but children shouldn't be allowed too close. Once the frothing has stopped, stir well to ensure that the bicarbonate of soda is well mixed, otherwise you may end up with salty bits in your honeycomb, then carefully pour it into the lined tray. Allow to cool before turning out and breaking into pieces. Store in an airtight container until needed.

To serve, top your dessert with some broken honeycomb and one of the rhubarb crisps and, if you are able to grow it, the angelica, which will add a little more magic to this dish.

Chef's note
If you want a very simple dessert, omit the jelly and serve the rhubarb compote with whipped cream or Crème Chantilly (see page 156) instead of the custard.

PEAS

'A TINY

TENDER GARDEN PEA is exquisite, with a flavour and aroma that is the pure essence of spring,' says Raymond. 'When the pea plants flower, the taller varieties in particular give a real beauty to the garden and in my kitchen we love to use the flowers and shoots almost as much as the peas. When I had my first restaurant in Oxford, before I had a kitchen garden, we would finish at one in the morning, and a few hours later, I would be out with my young team of chefs in the fields of the local pick-your-own farm.

Shelling peas and varieties of mangetout entwine themselves around ornamental teepees in the garden at Kew.

'I'd be there with a huge basket, not to pick the peas or courgettes like everybody else; I wanted the shoots and flowers and seeds – this was 35 years ago, long before these became fashionable. People would look at me and think "crazy Frenchman".'

There are three main types of pea in the *Pisum* genus of the pea family. The field pea is grown for its dried seeds (i.e. the peas inside) – the pods are left to dry on the plant and then the yellowy-grey peas are harvested and stored like pulses, so they need to be soaked to soften them before cooking. Then there are the two types of fresh pea (*Pisum sativum*): shelling peas, cultivated for the immature green seeds (the little green orbs that we are most familiar with); and edible podded varieties, such as mangetout and sugar snap peas.

In the Kew garden shelling peas and mangetout entwine themselves around bamboo canes which are tied together at the top to form teepees. 'The tall heritage varieties produce an amazing collection of flowers in different shades of pink and purple,' says Alice. 'The heritage Blackdown Blue pea and Carouby de Maussane mangetout, with their lavender flowers, look particularly stunning, and one of the pea varieties, Ezethas Krombek Blauwschok, has lovely pink–purple flowers and purple pods, which look very dramatic when you open them and see the green peas inside.' Carouby de Maussane is a favourite heritage variety of Raymond's which comes from near Avignon in France, while Blackdown Blue has a history as colourful as its flowers. The story goes that during the First World War a young soldier returning from the battlefields of the Somme was given a bag of French peas as a memento of happier times. He took them home with him to Somerset where his family and friends have been growing them ever since.

It is thought that field peas originated in western Asia, where archaeological evidence shows that they were being eaten from as long ago as 9000–8000BC. In Britain samples have been excavated in Glastonbury dating back to the Iron Age. In the Middle Ages, peas were an invaluable subsistence crop, which could be stored easily and boiled up to make a wholesome if stodgy pease porridge or pudding, maybe with a bit of bacon, if it was to be had.

At the end of the fourteenth century, however, a new style of fresh or 'garden' pea started to take Europe by storm. In Italy a dwarf variety began to be grown, known as *piselli novella*. When Catherine de Medici married Henry II of France in 1533, she is reputed to have brought a whole host of foods with her, including these novelty peas which the French named *petit pois*. Their status as a brief seasonal luxury rather than a peasant staple continued all the way through the seventeenth century. Louis XIV was said to be especially fond of them, and Françoise d'Aubigné, Madame de Maintenon, who became Louis's second wife, even wrote of the obsession with peas in one of her letters to him. 'The subject of peas continues to absorb all others, the anxiety to eat them, the pleasure of having eaten them, and the desire to eat them again, are the three great matters which have been discussed by our princes for four days past. Some ladies, even after having supped at the royal table and well supped too, returning to their own homes, at the risk of suffering from indigestion, will again eat peas before going to bed. It is both a fashion and a madness.'

When Charles II was restored to the English throne in 1660 after his exile at Louis's court, this fashion for 'posh' peas followed him, and

Above: The pea variety Ezethas Krombek Blauwschok has deep purple pods which contrast dramatically with the vivid green peas inside.

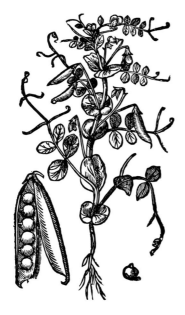

Historically peas have an importance that goes way beyond their culinary use: Gregor Mendel, known as the father of modern genetic science, used the garden pea in his studies.

the fresh garden style became a status symbol amongst the aristocracy: one up on 'poor' dried peas, which continued to be a staple for ordinary folk throughout Georgian times.

In the early nineteenth century, when the process of canning was first developed, garden peas were one of the earliest vegetables to undergo the new conservation treatment. The first tins were time-consuming and expensive to produce and so canned foods were only accessible to the moneyed and aspiring classes. However, as smaller, machine-made tins became available they gradually became more affordable, and so the idea of fresh 'posh' peas and 'poor' conserved peas finally came together in a cheap, nutritious store cupboard food that everyone could enjoy.

'And you know I have to pay tribute to the invention of the process of freezing peas a century and a half or so later,' says Raymond. 'We should not be snobbish or cheffy about frozen peas. The peas can harvested and frozen within a few hours, which minimises the loss of nutrients, so they are a magnificent way of feeding billions of people in a healthy way.'

Historically, peas have also played an important role in the world of genetics, since in the 1860s the Austrian monk, Gregor Mendel, credited as the father of modern genetic science, famously used the garden pea for his studies, crossing different strains and observing the results. Mendel looked at the colour of the pods, flowers and seeds, the position of the flowers on the stem and stem length, and also investigated the fact that some peas appeared wrinkled inside the pod, while others were round – and the wrinkled ones were sweeter. Over a century later, plant scientists at the John Innes Centre for microbial science built on Mendel's work and established that wrinkled peas were lacking a starch-branching enzyme which meant that they converted less of their sugars into starch and were therefore sweeter than round ones. The higher sugar content allowed the wrinkled peas to absorb more water as they grew, so the skins stretched but then shrivelled as the peas matured. The round peas, containing less sugar and more starch, were able to take up less water, so their skins didn't stretch and they held their shape. All of this research has enabled growers to develop strains of pea with a good balance of flavour and sweetness, for example the double-podded Hurst Green Shaft, being grown alongside the heritage varieties at Kew.

GROWING NOTES

Fresh peas are divided into shelling peas and edible-podded varieties of mangetout and sugar snap peas. As the names suggest, shelling peas are grown only for the seeds (peas) inside, and the pods are discarded, whereas the edible-podded ones are eaten whole.

Like potatoes, shelling peas can be early or maincrop. Early varieties can be harvested in around 11–13 weeks after sowing while maincrop varieties will take around 15 weeks.

While most peas need to be sown in fairly warm temperatures, sometime between March and June, some of the hardy varieties of shelling pea being grown at Kew, such as the low-growing Douce Provence and Feltham First, can also be sown in mid-October to November if the weather is mild. These grow over winter and produce an early harvest from May onwards.

In the autumn/winter before planting, dig some rotted manure into beds that are in a sunny area of the garden or have dappled shade.

Edible-podded varieties are sown at the same time as shelling peas. Mangetout are best harvested while the pods are still flat, whereas sugar snap peas should be left until semi-mature, when the peas inside the pods are beginning to swell.

Shelling peas are often divided into 'wrinkle-seeded' varieties, which tend to be sweeter, and 'smooth-seeded' types, which are often hardier but contain less sugar.

Although peas (including mangetout and sugar snap peas) can be sown directly into the ground, mice love them and will ravage the tiny plants given a chance, so ideally start off your seeds during February/March in a greenhouse or on a windowsill. Peas produce quite long roots, so to avoid disturbing them when you transplant them to the garden, rather than planting in pots, use trays of deep modules, or 'root trainers', which open out like a book. Or, if you happen to have a length of drainpipe to hand, you could cut it in half lengthways and use each half as a container for planting, which will allow you to just slide off the seedlings into the beds later. Push the seed no deeper than 5cm into compost, cover with more compost and water in.

Plant out the seedlings when they are 15–20cm tall, no higher, as the more top growth, the more stress they will feel when transplanted.

The growing peas will need to be supported. For low-growing varieties, you can just use hazel pea sticks. Taller varieties can be supported by runs of canes with netting stretched across them, however they look most beautiful supported by cane teepees as at Kew.

For the tallest varieties you will need canes of about 2.5m for your teepees. 'Put them in before planting, to avoid disturbing the roots later,' says Joe. 'Place your canes in a circle, spacing them out evenly at around 15cm intervals, then tie them together at their tops. It is a good idea to put in some little hazel pea sticks or twigs between each cane, so that as the plants grow, their tendrils can latch on to them.'

Once the teepees are in position, plant your peas in a single or double circle of drills (furrows made in the soil) around the outside

Left and above: At Kew the pea seedlings are planted around teepees made with canes.

of the canes – the drills need to be 4–5cm deep and the seedlings roughly 5cm apart.

Keep the bed weed free and do not overwater before the plants flower, as this encourages more leaf production. Once the flowers appear, water will help the pods to develop and swell

All peas need to be harvested regularly to encourage more pods to be produced. The pods on the lower part of the plants will mature first, so begin harvesting these and work your way up as the pods mature. 'If you stop harvesting, the plant will stop producing.' says Joe.

Late in the season the leaves of maincrop varieties can be affected by mildew, which causes them to discolour or turn yellow, especially if the plants are growing in a damp environment. Remove affected leaves and avoid overhead watering.

At the end of the season cut back leaves and stems, which can be composted. Dig in the roots which will break down and release nitrogen into the soil for a crop of a different vegetable to be grown in the same space the following year.

RAYMOND'S FLAVOUR NOTES

I love peas especially when they are tiny; oval and barely formed. It is very wasteful, I know – a total indulgence, but for the gourmand, pure heaven. They are so sweet and tender; you only need 10 seconds' cooking to soften them. By the middle of the season they are perfect, but beware of old, end of season peas that will be floury and tough and will lose colour when you cook them.

I always cook peas using the 'emulsion' method on page 17.

SPRING PEA RISOTTO

Fresh, sweet peas combined with the luxurious fat grain of the rice makes for an exceptional spring dish, with just enough heartiness if the weather isn't yet that warm. The variety of pea I chose for this dish was Feltham First, which is a long-standing British favourite – a low-growing, early variety that produces lovely sweet, but not too sweet, peas. Rather than using a chicken or vegetable stock, I wanted to try making it just with the pea pods to intensify the flavour – and also because I never forget my mother's mantra, 'thou shalt not waste'! But during this process I discovered something very interesting. The first time I made the stock I chopped and puréed the raw pods and then added water – but the taste, oh it was horrible – soapy and bitter! Intuitively I thought it must be enzymes within the flavour compound, so I tried again and this time I blanched my pea pods in boiling water for about 40 seconds, hoping to remove the bitterness. I cooled them down, chopped and puréed them, then I made my stock. And it worked like a dream; it had a beautiful clean pea flavour.

Yet, I wanted to know exactly why this chemical reaction had happened. I contacted a wonderful scientist friend, George Oakland, who did some research and discovered that the culprit was the flavour/aroma compound, pyrazine. It is also found in some wines, such as Sauvignon Blanc and some Bordeaux. Pea pods contain quite a lot of pyrazine and its harsh, raw vegetal flavour was coming through in the cooking process. By blanching the raw pods for just 40 seconds, you neutralise the compounds. I still find it so fascinating and extraordinary that one small process can change the flavour so completely.

SERVES 4–6

Preparation time: 10 minutes
Cooking time: 40 minutes

For the pea stock (makes 600ml)
350g fresh pea pods, shelled (use the shells for the stock and the peas for the purée and vegetables)
350ml iced water

For the pea purée
100g fresh peas (shelled weight)
10g unsalted butter
pinch of sea salt

Start by making the pea stock, in a large pan of simmering water, blanch the pea pod shells for 1 minute. Using a slotted spoon, remove the blanched shells and refresh them in the iced water. (By refreshing the pods in the iced water you not only retain the colour but also the freshness and maximise the retention of vitamins and nutrients.)

Once cooled, blitz the iced water and blanched pea pods in a food processor until smooth and strain through a fine sieve. Set aside 100ml to make the pea purée and the remaining 500ml to make the risotto.

Next, make the pea purée. In a small saucepan on a medium heat, sweat the peas in the butter for 5 minutes, adding a pinch of salt. Add the 100ml of reserved pea stock, bring to a boil and simmer for 4 minutes. Transfer to a blender or food processor, blend until smooth and leave to cool.

Continued overleaf $\rightarrow$

For the risotto

½ white onion, diced

2 tbsp refined olive oil or 30g
    unsalted butter

1 small garlic clove, finely grated

200g carnaroli rice

100ml white wine, plus extra to
    finish (optional)

40g freshly grated Parmesan

sea salt and freshly ground black
    pepper

For the vegetables

5g unsalted butter

120g baby courgettes, cut into
    2mm slices

140g fresh peas (podded weight)

40g French breakfast radish,
    sliced

40g radish tops

40g baby leaf spinach

To finish

juice of ¼ lemon

50ml extra virgin olive oil or 50g
    unsalted butter

To garnish (optional)

15g pea shoots, blanched in
    boiling water for 5 seconds

20g Parmesan shavings

For the risotto, in a medium saucepan on a low heat, sweat the onion in the olive oil with a pinch of salt for 2 minutes, until translucent. Add the garlic. Stir in the rice and continue to cook on a low heat for 3 minutes, until the grains of rice appear shiny (this will give flavour and prevent them sticking together).

Pour in the white wine, then the 500ml of reserved pea stock, stir and bring to the gentlest simmer with only one bubble breaking the surface every minute. Season with salt and pepper then cover with a lid and leave to cook for 20 minutes. Check every now and again that it is not boiling.

After 20 minutes of cooking, pick up a grain of rice. You will see a tiny speck of white starch in the middle – this means the risotto is nearly cooked. Now you need to add the creaminess that we love so much in a risotto and that means 5 minutes of hard and fast stirring. By beating the rice, each grain will rub against another, which will extract the starch and give the rice its beautifully creamy consistency. Stir in 200ml of the cooled pea purée, which will revive the colour and add freshness. Stir in the Parmesan, taste and correct the seasoning. Set aside.

Prepare the vegetables. In a small saucepan on a high heat, bring the butter, 50ml of water and a pinch of salt to the boil. Add the courgettes, cover with a lid and cook on a high heat for 30 seconds, then add the peas, radishes, radish tops and spinach, cover again and continue for 20 seconds.

To finish the risotto, stir in the lemon juice, olive oil or butter and maybe a dash of white wine to sharpen the flavour. Taste and adjust the seasoning. You can serve the risotto in a large dish topped with the vegetables, blanched pea shoots and a few shavings of Parmesan, if using, or in four large bowls.

Chef's note

I developed this technique of cooking a risotto as a means of saving time. I hated watching my chefs spend so long stirring the rice. My method requires less time and effort but every grain of rice is perfectly cooked. Those last 5 minutes are crucial. By stirring you work the starch and extract it, which is what gives the risotto its hallmark creaminess.

LAMB'S LIVER WITH PEA PUREE

The purée here is a take on the British favourite, mushy peas, but made with fresh, sweet peas. Visually I like the contrast of the matt look of the purée and the crushed peas and chopped herbs, which have extra virgin olive oil mixed through them to give a silky shine.

SERVES 4

Preparation time: 10 minutes
Cooking time: 35 minutes

For the braised onions
160g grelot onions, peeled and
    halved
1 thyme sprig
2 black peppercorns
4 tsp extra virgin olive oil
500ml water
sea salt and freshly ground black
    pepper

For the pea purée
40g white onion, finely diced
25g unsalted butter
125g peas, podded
100ml boiling water

For the crushed peas
200g shelled peas
100ml water
1 mint sprig, chopped
1 marjoram sprig, chopped
4 tsp extra virgin olive oil

For the liver
350g lamb's liver, washed, dried
    and cut on an angle into 2cm-
    thick slices
30g unsalted butter
50ml water
½ 'new season' garlic clove,
    crushed

For the braised onions, in a small saucepan on a medium heat, mix the onions, thyme, black peppercorns, olive oil, water and a tiny pinch of salt. Cover with a lid and cook on a gentle simmer for 15 minutes, until soft but holding their shape. Leave to cool at room temperature in their liquid. Once cooled, pat dry with a clean cloth, place back in a clean pan and set aside until ready to reheat.

For the pea purée, in a medium saucepan on a medium heat, gently sweat the onions in the butter with a pinch of salt and pepper for 5 minutes until they are soft and translucent. Increase the heat to high, add the peas and boiling water, and bring to a rapid boil for 3 minutes (if using older peas, for 5 minutes), covered. Transfer to a blender and blend the peas and all the cooking juices on full speed for 1 minute, until smooth and velvety. Transfer the purée to a small saucepan and set aside.

For the crushed peas, in a small pan on a high heat, place the peas, water, mint and marjoram and bring to the boil for 2 minutes. Drain, refresh in ice cold water and crush with a fork. In a small bowl, mix the crushed peas, oil, two pinches of salt and a pinch of pepper. Taste and correct the seasoning.

To cook the liver, first season it with two pinches of salt and a pinch of pepper. In a medium frying pan over a medium–high heat, warm the butter until foaming and cook the seasoned liver for 3 minutes on each side. Use a temperature probe to ensure a core temperature of 70°C is achieved, then remove the cooked livers from the pan and leave to rest for 5 minutes on a warm plate in a warm place; the core temperature will continue to rise to 72°C. Meanwhile, add the water and garlic to the pan used for the livers. Taste, season with salt and pepper. Return it to a

Continued overleaf →

To serve

20 pea shoot sprigs

medium heat, bring to a boil and stir with a spatula to capture all the wonderful roasting juices and flavours.

To serve, reheat the pea purée, crushed peas and braised onions. Place a spoonful of the purée in the centre of each plate, add two generous spoonfuls of the crushed peas and the braised onions. Place the rested liver on top, arrange the peas shoots on top and finish by dressing the dish with the roasting juices and scattering them around the plate.

Chef's note

Campylobacter is a dangerous bacteria present in all offal. To kill it and ensure safe food hygiene, the liver needs to be cooked to 70°C for a minimum of 3 minutes on each side. You may lose the mellow quality of a medium liver, but you're safe!

Variations

You could easily use broad beans instead of the peas.

The lamb's liver could be replaced by sweetbreads.

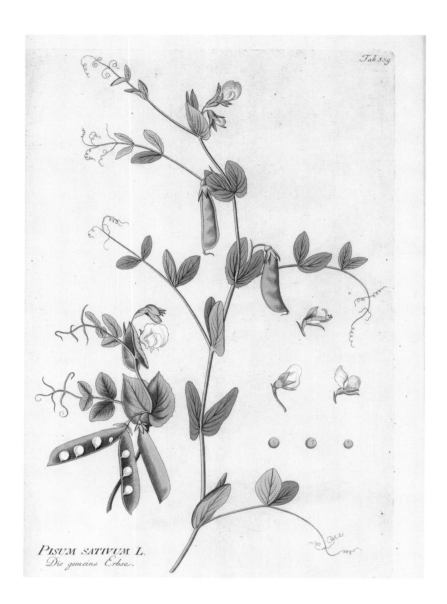

Tab. 559

PISUM SATIVUM L.
Die gemeine Erbse.

*Left: An engraving
of the pea plant*
(Pisum sativum) *from*
Icones Plantarum
Medicinalium, *vol. 6:
tab.559 (1788–1812),
a catalogue of around
700 medicinal plants
compiled by Austrian
physician Joseph
Jacob Plenck, a leading
figure in the history of
dermatology.*

ASPARAGUS

'FOR SO MANY OF US the vegetable that is most evocative of late spring, when the earth warms up, is asparagus,' says Raymond. 'Every time the first delicate spears appear it is a small miracle that never loses its fascination and mystery. It is like seeing a beautiful sunset. Even though we know that sunsets have happened for millions of years, we are still in awe.'

The Romans were so enamoured of asparagus that they employed runners and chariots to transport the spears up into the Alps, where they used ice and snow to store and preserve them.

A member of the lily family, asparagus has been harvested in the wild for thousands of years and is depicted on Egyptian tombs dating from 4000BC. The Ancient Greeks valued it for its medicinal properties. Dioscorides, a first-century Greek physician, recommended extracts of asparagus root for treatment of urinary and kidney problems, jaundice and sciatica, and John Gerard, who published his famous *The Herball* in 1597 (an original is in the Library Collection at Kew), noted that it was thought to 'increase seed and stir up lust'. Certainly they weren't wrong about the nutritional values, as asparagus is indeed rich in folic acid, fibre, potassium and provitamin A.

The Romans especially appear to have loved asparagus. Cato the Elder gave a detailed account of how to grow it in *De Agricultura*, and one of the earliest recipes for asparagus tips appears in the collection of Roman recipes dating back almost 2,000 years, known as *Apicius De Re Coquinaria*, possibly named after the gourmet Marcus Gavius Apicius, though no one knows for sure. It involves asparagus tips pounded with black pepper, lovage, coriander, savoury, onion, wine, liquamen (fermented fish sauce) and oil. Eggs are added, and then the dish is baked. The Romans knew how to preserve foods using snow and ice in underground pits, and it is said that chariots and runners would transport asparagus up to the Alps, where the freezing temperatures would allow the spears to be stored for months.

In Raymond's region, Franche-Comté, the most wooded part of France, a favourite – and often lucrative – childhood pastime was going out in search of wild asparagus. 'You could walk tens of miles and not find anything, because wild asparagus needs three conditions to grow: a combe (hollow), light and moisture. Then suddenly you would see a shaft of sunlight beaming through the trees, run towards it and the combe would be revealed. Below you were thousands of spears, their little heads stretching up to the sun, their feet in water. It was always a marvellous, magical moment. We would cut as many of the spears as we could and tie them in bundles, then find some hazelnut branches and string the bunches to them, so that we could carry our treasure home on our shoulders – at least 30 bundles hanging from each branch. We would be feeling very rich, because we could sell some to local restaurants for pocket money, and keep the rest for my mother to blanch in boiling water. We would eat the asparagus warm (never too hot, or too cold, or you kill the flavour) with a simple vinaigrette.'

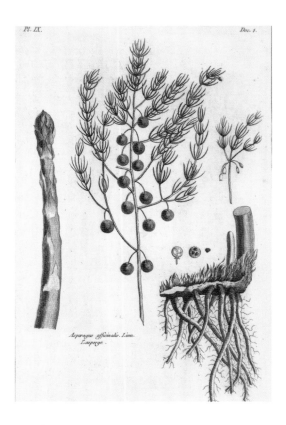

Pl. IX.   *Dec. 1.*

Asparagus officinalis. Linn.
Larpeyre.

Opposite: Asparagus fronds, also depicted (above) in this engraving of Asparagus officinalis *from the* Histoire Universelle du Règne Végétal, *vol. 11: t.9 (1775–78) by the French physician, lawyer and botanist, Pierre Joseph Buchoz.*

As far as cultivated asparagus goes, Raymond reveals he had never seen green asparagus before coming to England. 'At first it was a cultural shock because in France asparagus was always white. Ours was not an asparagus-growing region, so we only saw the thick white spears conserved in jars. These were very expensive, so we would have them as a treat at Christmas with citrus mayonnaise. Beautiful. Now, the world has changed and you can see green asparagus in the markets in France, and some speciality white asparagus is being grown in England.'

White and green asparagus are the same plant, but grown quite differently. The shoots of green asparagus emerge into the light and develop their colour through photosynthesis, while the shoots of white asparagus are kept covered in soil, so that they grow in the dark and stay white. 'What is fascinating,' says Raymond, 'is that when you exclude the light to "force" rhubarb (see page 41) or blanch chicory (see page 226) these become more tender, so you would also expect the same of white asparagus. But no, it is just the opposite. You have to peel off the outer layer of a spear of white asparagus very well, as this is fibrous and bitter, and you must cook the spears for much longer.' According to Paula Rudall, scientist at the Jodrell Laboratory at Kew, although the process of photosynthesis is common in each case, 'we eat different parts of each plant. Asparagus is a young growing shoot (stem plus leaves), whereas the edible part of the rhubarb, for example, is the fleshy petiole (stalk) of the leaf'. So the effect on texture is different.

'On a more emotional level, asparagus is hugely symbolic for me,' says Raymond. 'When I first came to England there was a stiffness and a protocol about eating in restaurants, which I so wanted to replace with the idea I had grown up with – that the table brings friends and family together to relax, share and enjoy good food. Then one day I watched a young girl and her mother eating at my restaurant and the girl was picking up the asparagus spears with her fingers and biting into them, under the disapproving eye of *maman*. I wanted to jump for joy.'

Left: String threaded around bamboo stakes offers support to the flimsy asparagus fronds.

GROWING NOTES

Asparagus prefers an open, sunny place, but doesn't mind dappled shade. It does need well-draining soil, though.

You need to be patient. Although there are newer varieties that can produce a crop more quickly, as a general rule an asparagus crown has to be three years old before you can harvest your first full crop. After that, it can carry on producing for 20 years or so.

As with rhubarb, it is best to plant one-year-old crowns. These are either male or female, 'but choose male ones which grow more vigorously and can't self-seed and pop up randomly as the female ones can,' advises Joe.

Prepare the soil well before planting. Remove all weeds, dig a trench 30cm wide and 20cm deep, add some well-rotted manure or compost and cover with 5cm of the excavated soil.

Using some more of the excavated soil, make a ridge about 10cm high all the way along the centre of the trench and place the crowns at 35–45cm intervals on top. Spread out the roots as evenly as you can from the centre of the crown (see pictures above and opposite). 'We like to sprinkle on some Soil Association-certified organic chicken manure pellets at this point, which is a very good slow-release fertiliser,' says Joe. Cover with soil, banking it up a little, to the top of the crown, leaving the tips of the buds just poking through. Water in and add a layer of compost to retain moisture in the soil.

When the first shoots (fronds) come through, they will be quite flimsy, so it is good to put in some bamboo stakes and thread a border of

string around them ready to support the shoots as they grow.

Watch out for stripy asparagus beetles. 'They look very beautiful, but they rasp away and strip off the outer layer of the parts of the plants that are above ground, so they turn yellow and die,' says Alice. 'If you see the beetles, you need to pick them off and squash them.'

Don't harvest the spears in the two seasons after planting but let the fern-like top growth flourish to strengthen the crown. When it turns yellow in the autumn, it can be cut down to just above soil level.

In year three harvest the spears lightly, cutting only a few with a sharp knife, just below soil level. Cut back the yellowing top growth in autumn as before.

In the seasons that follow you can harvest as many asparagus spears as you like, but not for more than around 6–8 weeks. In England the spears are traditionally harvested between the end of April and Midsummer's Day, the 21st June.

RAYMOND'S FLAVOUR NOTES

The French prefer white asparagus, the English prefer green and they have completely different flavours and textures.

With Joe I planted a high-yielding, green, early-season variety of asparagus called Gijnlim, which is also grown for my restaurant kitchen by a specialist grower on a local farm – it has an amazing flavour. The key is to cook green asparagus as soon as possible after harvesting as it loses its intensity of flavour very quickly. A really fresh spear should snap, not bend, so handle it carefully, like crystal. And if you rub the spears together, they should sing. I once played a symphony on asparagus in a French market and drew quite a crowd. But wouldn't you know, when I tried to show off my 'musical' talent in front of the TV cameras, the asparagus refused to sing!

Green asparagus can be steamed, blanched then char-grilled, or cooked in the traditional way in boiling water very quickly (this is one of the few times I boil a vegetable, because it is for a very short time), for 6–8 minutes. Because the cooking time is so short, there is no need to keep the tips out of the water.

If you come across white asparagus you will need to peel the spears very well and they can take up to 40 minutes to cook, so you do have to stand them upright and keep the tips out of the water so that these don't become soggy.

ASPARAGUS AND HOLLANDAISE SAUCE

Along with new potatoes, asparagus is one of the most prized spring vegetables and marks the beginning of the season. There is nothing more exciting than seeing those first heads bursting through the soil. Asparagus is very at home with two great classic sauces: hollandaise and mayonnaise, both of which I've included here. I can assure you that this hollandaise will not punish you in the way that a more traditional recipe might – it will be the lightest you will have tasted, containing only 50g of butter for four guests.

SERVES 4

Preparation time: 5 minutes
Cooking time: 20 minutes

For the asparagus
20 green asparagus spears, woody
   ends removed

For the hollandaise
3 medium egg yolks
100ml water
50g unsalted butter, melted
pinch sea salt
juice of ¼ lemon

Prepare the asparagus, using the tip of a sharp knife, remove the leaves and peel the ends.

For the hollandaise, prepare a bain marie (i.e. a saucepan of barely-simmering water over a low heat). In a bowl set over the bain marie, whisk the egg yolks and water vigorously. As you whisk, you partly cook the sauce as well as bringing in lots of air bubbles and creating an emulsion. After about 10 minutes, you should have a beautifully expanded, light and lemon-coloured foam, about six or seven times its original volume. Pour in the melted butter and whisk briefly. Season with the salt and lemon juice and taste to correct the seasoning if necessary.

To cook the asparagus, the best way is to steam it as this will help it to better retain its flavour, colour and nutrients; it will take about 7 minutes on full steam. Alternatively, boil the asparagus for the same amount of time. Drain the asparagus on to a cloth then arrange on a serving dish. Either serve the hollandaise separately or spoon it over the spears.

Variation with mayonnaise
All the ingredients should be at room temperature. Put 2 medium egg yolks into a large bowl. Add 2 teaspoons of Dijon mustard and very gradually whisk in 200ml of vegetable or rapeseed oil. The egg yolk contains lecithin, which will absorb the oil and create the perfect emulsion, provided you add the oil slowly. If it separates, either your oil is too cold or you added it too quickly. If so, move the mayonnaise to one side of the bowl and start to whisk in a little warm water in circles. If it is completely split, do the same using a little mustard, which also contains lecithin. Thin the emulsion with a tablespoon of lemon juice and season. Stir in a tablespoon of crème fraîche, taste and adjust the seasoning and thin further with water if necessary.

GRILLED ASPARAGUS WITH VEGETABLE CRUMBLE

Asparagus served in the classic way, with mayonnaise or hollandaise sauce (see the previous recipe) is hard to beat, but what I was trying to do with this new dish was to mix the flavours of the spring with the warmer flavours and textures of the summer. I've spiced things up a little with the slight smokiness that comes from griddling or barbecuing asparagus, a large sprinkling of smoked paprika and a hint of chilli.

SERVES 4

Preparation time: 5 minutes
Cooking time: 25 minutes

For the paprika dressing
3 tbsp extra virgin olive oil
½ tsp smoked paprika
2 tsp lemon juice

For the hard-boiled eggs and grilled asparagus
2 eggs
20 green asparagus spears, woody ends removed
90–120ml refined olive oil

For the vegetable crumble
3 tbsp olive oil
80g baby courgettes (about 2½), pulsed in a food processor for 30 seconds
80g cauliflower, pulsed in a food processor for 30 seconds
30g banana shallot, finely diced
½ red chilli, finely chopped
3 large pinches of smoked paprika
pinch of salt
80ml water
2 tbsp lemon juice
10g parsley, chopped
5g chives, chopped

For the paprika dressing, mix all the ingredients and reserve.

To hard-boil the eggs, using a spoon, slide the eggs gently into a small pan of water. Bring to a simmer for 13 minutes, then remove and immediately run under cold water. While still warm, peel the eggs then transfer to the fridge. Once cold, separate the whites from the yolks and grate each part on the coarse side of the grater (keep them separated), then set aside.

To prepare the asparagus, lay five spears side by side and secure them together with two metal skewers (thread these through one at each end, avoiding the tips, so that the spears are kept straight). Repeat with the remaining three batches of five. Blanch in plenty of boiling water for 3 minutes, then immediately plunge them into cold water to stop the cooking and dry thoroughly (leave them on the skewers).

To cook the asparagus, heat a griddle pan on a high heat. Brush the skewered spears lightly with 2 tablespoons of the olive oil. When the pan is hot, lay the asparagus flat and leave for 3 minutes to gain deep griddle marks. Turn over using tongs and griddle for another 3 minutes. If necessary do the griddling in batches; simply keep the asparagus warm in an oven set at 80°C/Gas ¼ while you grill the remaining asparagus.

For the vegetable crumble, in a large sauté pan on a high heat, add the olive oil and fry the courgette, cauliflower, shallot, chilli, paprika and salt for 30 seconds. Add the water, lemon juice, parsley, chives and egg white and boil for 5 seconds then remove from the heat. Stir in the egg yolk and check the seasoning.

To serve, place a spoonful of the vegetable crumble in the centre of each plate and arrange a stack of the grilled asparagus on top. Finish with a drizzle of the paprika dressing.

45

Turpin P.

Lambert F. sculp

ASPERGE.

Asparagus officinalis *as depicted in* Flore médicale décrite, *vol 1: pl.45 (1815–20), a work by the French physician and botanist, François-Pierre Chaumeton.*

BEANS

THE KITCHEN GARDEN at Kew was planned with splendour in mind, not only in terms of freshness, flavour and organic and heritage values, but through the beauty of the plants themselves, and few crops contribute as generously as beans.

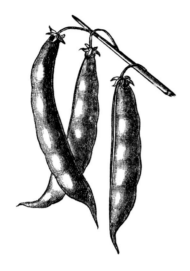

Hugging every ornamental pillar in summer is a Scarlet Emperor runner bean laden with vivid red flowers; while climbing French beans, whose pods are rounded, sleek, slimmer and usually shorter than the flat runner beans, are entwined around tall teepees created with bamboo canes. Amongst them is Borlotto Lingua di Fuoco – 'tongues of fire,' so called because of the red flame-like streaks across its pods; and Kew Blue, with its purpley-red stems, purpley-pink flowers and stunning deep purpley-blue pods, said to have originated in the Royal Botanic Gardens, and now available to growers through the Heritage Seed Library. The library, of which Raymond is a long-time supporter and vice president, is maintained by the charity Garden Organic and is dedicated to conserving and perpetuating old and rare varieties.

Many of these ancient seeds have intriguing stories to tell. Particularly poignant is that of the Trail of Tears beans. These are named after the handfuls that were carried by the last Cherokee Indians as they were driven out of Georgia and Tennessee by President Andrew Jackson's administration to make way for white settlers. Thousands of the native Indians died along their 'trail of tears' as they made their way towards new settlements west of the Mississippi river, in what is now Oklahoma.

Then there is the heritage Lazy Housewife – the name perhaps not as derogatory as it might seem, as it is said to refer to the fact that this early nineteenth-century bean was the first French climbing bean to offer a stringless alternative to the runner bean, which was so much more fiddly to prepare. Not only that, but the plant is extremely prolific and the pods grow in clusters so they are easy to pick.

To add to the colour in the bean beds even further, Joe and Alice have interplanted the climbing beans with borage, which produces beautiful blue edible flowers, and is a nectar source for pollinating insects.

Of the broad beans, planted in an adjacent bed, the name of the heritage variety Crimson Flowered says it all. Grando Violetto produces green pods with stunning, flavoursome purple beans inside; Red Bristow has white flowers and red beans which maintain their colour when cooked; while Aquadulce Claudia, a heritage bean for autumn sowing, is a favourite, as it delivers succulent, tasty beans early in spring.

Opposite: Heritage varieties of bean frequently have stirring histories and evocative names, such as these colourful flame-streaked pods of Borlotto Lingua di Fuoco – 'tongues of fire' encasing delicately mottled beans.

Left: As the garden at Kew demonstrates, a fruit and vegetable plot can be a place of great beauty, and nothing adds more to the ornamental nature of the garden than a profusion of flowering, climbing beans.

HARICOT BEURRE.

Phadeolus vulgaris

Above: Illustration of a haricot bean, Phaseolus vulgaris, *from vol. 5, p.433 of a series published in 1849 by Louis van Houtte, entitled* Flore des serres et des jardins de l'Europe *(Flowers of the Greenhouses and Gardens of Europe).*

The Martock broad bean takes its name from the Somerset village of Martock, where it flourished in the loamy soil from the Middle Ages. A local saying recorded in the Somerset Record Office in the eighteenth century shows just how important it was in the local community: 'Take a Martock man by the collar and shake him, and you will hear the beans rattle in his belly'. However the variety was thought to have disappeared – only to be rediscovered in the 1970s to great delight, when it was found to be growing in the kitchen garden of the Bishop of Bath and Wells, who was offering samples in exchange for donations to the church roof restoration fund.

We tend not to think of Britain as having a rich culture of using dried beans, unlike many other European countries. But it was not always so. In the Middle Ages the pods would usually be left on the plant until dried and then the mature seeds inside, i.e. the beans, could be stored and reconstituted in pottages (thick soups). In the countryside, people who worked the fields often rose at sunrise and ate their main meal of the day late morning. Usually this would be some kind of pottage of beans to which they could add anything else they had in the way of vegetables, or a scrap of meat, to sustain them until sunset. Eventually though, as wheat to make bread became more accessible, dried beans fell out of favour.

Many of the varieties selected for the Kew garden were chosen to highlight the versatility in the life cycle of the bean. First the cook has the option of the whole pod, then the young fresh beans inside, and finally at the end of the season, the naturally dried beans.

'In my parents' garden we grew fine green beans for eating whole, but for the treasure inside, there were two varieties: Soisson flageolet and Lazy Housewife, which we called by the more respectful name of Coco. You know, I always thought that those beans were native to my region; I had no idea that in fact they are a German heritage variety. I used to help plant and water them, and put in the cane teepees to support them. We would let the pods swell and then eat some of the fresh grey Coco beans and green Soissons. What a beautiful flavour! My father would let the rest mature in their pods on the plant until they were dry, then harvest them and my mum would put them into sterilised jars and keep them in the cellar over winter.'

Broad beans, however, were a complete novelty to Raymond when he first arrived in England. 'In most of France we don't grow them at all,' he says. 'Only in the south-east where you have some of the greatest gardens; there they have a big reputation. But as soon as I discovered them I loved them, and they are so nutritious and full of protein, riboflavin and vitamin C. They must be small, though. In my first job as a head chef, the restaurant had a kitchen garden and a gardener, Mr Lay, a huge man who grew equally huge vegetables: the broad beans were fat and floury with thick skins and the runner beans were big, stringy and woody, so you had to peel both sides.

I wanted young sweet broad beans and I wanted the shoots and flowers too, as well as mangetout and French climbing beans. But when this young, skinny little Frenchman told the head gardener in broken English that things were going to change significantly, he didn't like me at all. So late at night, well after evening service, when it was dark, I used to sneak into the garden and pick the vegetables when they were small. Like Peter Rabbit, I was listening for the sound of rustling in case the gardener was around and would catch me. I remember one time I saw the shadow of him behind me and I ran and ran. Thank God the skinny little Frenchman could run faster than the enormous English gardener!'

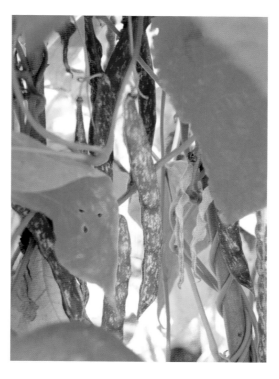

Left: The magnificent colours of so many heritage varieties of bean turn a vegetable into a veritable artwork.

GROWING NOTES

FRENCH CLIMBING BEANS AND RUNNER BEANS

Plant two seeds at a time into pots of compost around the end of March/beginning of April and keep them under glass or on a window ledge until they form their first true leaves. Once the frosts are over, you will need to 'harden off' the plants for a week, to get them used to the change in temperature before planting in the garden. Do this by putting them out in a cold frame, if you have one, leaving the greenhouse door open, or putting the pots outside (but bring them in if there is a chance of overnight frost).

Dig in some well-rotted manure or compost in advance, and as for planting peas (see page 58), erect some bamboo canes to form teepees. You don't need to put in any small twigs as beans don't produce clinging tendrils in the same way.

With a trowel, make a hole at the base of each cane and put in one plant by each, so that the top of the root ball is level with the surrounding soil. Fill around the root with soil and firm in place using your fingers.

Water in well and, if you like, add a 5cm deep layer of compost, which will help keep the moisture in the soil.

'Climbing beans will usually take hold of the teepee canes by themselves but tie them if necessary,' says Alice.

BROAD BEANS

These like well-drained, sheltered gardens, but are hardy and easy to grow, with minimum attention. Sow early-cropping varieties such as Aquadulce Claudia and Express around November, and summer-cropping varieties such as Crimson Flowered, Grando Violetto and Martock in March.

Dig in some well-rotted manure or garden compost before sowing and make sure you dig the soil deeply as the plants have long roots.

Sow the seeds individually, about 11cm apart, in double rows, allowing about 22cm between the rows. If you are sowing a series of double rows, allow a space of just under a metre in between each double row.

Stretch a length of string around some canes along the outside of the rows so that the plants have something to support them as they grow.

Once you can see that the plants are well established and healthy 'thin out' the rows by pulling up every other plant. 'It is a traditional failsafe to sow the plants this densely to start with,' says Alice, 'as with all heritage varieties you can't be sure that every seed will germinate, so if you sow more plants than you need, you are pretty sure to get a good crop. Don't be tempted to leave them all – if the plants are too congested you run the risk of limiting your crop and encouraging disease'.

The most common broad bean pest is the black bean aphid, or blackfly, which is sap-sucking and will go for the juiciest young parts of the plant. This weakens the plant and the aphids can also carry viruses. 'Either squish them when you see them, or if there are many of them, spray with soapy water to kill them,' says Joe. 'When the plant is nearing full height you can nip out the very top new growth, which is where they tend to gather.' You might also try planting summer savory around the beans as it is said to ward off the aphids, and its thyme-y flavour also makes a good addition to the cooked beans.

Like peas, the bean pods mature from the bottom of the plant upwards, so harvest accordingly (in May and June for beans sown in the autumn, and throughout the rest of the summer for those planted in spring) before the pods grow too big.

Above left: The red flowers of the Scarlet Emperor runner bean, as well as broad bean flowers (above, right) are a lovely addition to salads.

RAYMOND'S FLAVOUR NOTES

There are six varieties of climbing French bean in the garden at Kew. While some beans are dual purpose and can be enjoyed whole or allowed to grow on to develop the beans inside, most are best for one or the other.

For young French beans to be eaten whole, one of my favourite varieties is Eva. A really fresh green bean should be crisp and snap sharply in half. I like to cook them using my emulsion method (see page 17).

For the beans inside the pods, which can be eaten fresh or dried, the ones that are close to my heart are Lazy Housewife (Coco), which I grew up with (my best bean experience!); Soissons (a flageolet variety); and Tarbais, from Tarbes in the South of France, which is the traditional bean for cassoulet. The beans of all these are beautiful, creamy and tasty.

Then there are the borlotto varieties, whose mottled pink shells encase the borlotti beans inside. Fresh borlotti beans are wonderful simmered with some herbs and garlic for about 25 minutes until tender, then dressed simply with oil and some salt and pepper. Lovely warm or at room temperature in salads. Or if you let the beans dry, you can store them. Soak them overnight before cooking, perhaps with some spicy chorizo sausage and cabbage.

Runner beans such as Czar can be eaten young and green, but you can also leave the pods to dry on the plant so the big white beans form inside, then cook them like butter beans.

Of the broad beans, favourites which arrive early in the season are the hardy heritage Aquadulce Claudia and Crimson Flowered, which have flavourful, but relatively small beans, and then in midsummer, Express, whose beans are succulent and juicy.

When it comes to broad beans, I know that chefs can't resist taking the tiniest beans and slipping off the outer skins, because of course inside they are a bright, beautiful emerald green – but I find this quite ridiculous because a very young bean has no flavour. Wait at least until it is adolescent, please! And then leave the skins on. When the beans are tender and sweet you keep so much more flavour and texture by leaving them whole, and really, who has the time to peel them? It only makes sense to peel a broad bean when it is quite large and the skin is beginning to toughen.

Right: Kidney bean, Phaseolus compressus lucasianus (*as it was known in the ninetheenth century*) *from* Flore des Serres et des Jardins de l'Europe, *vol. 17 (1845), Louis van Houtte (see page 86).*

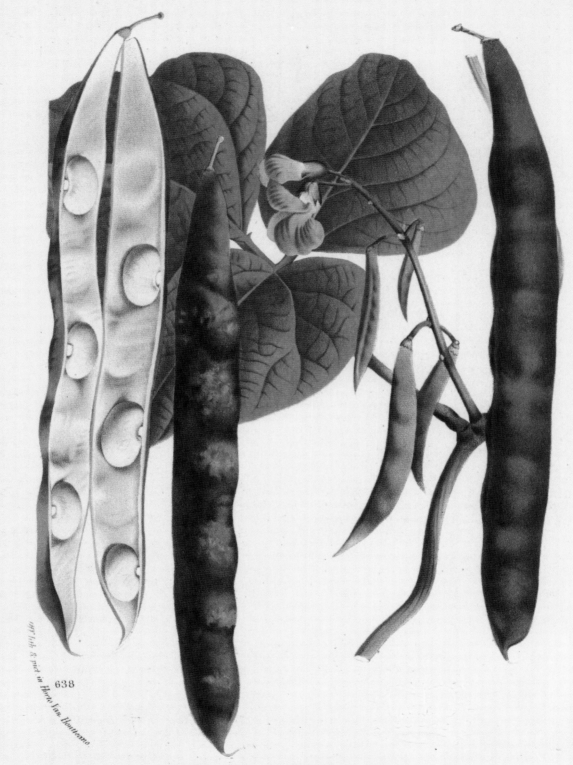

PHASEOLUS ~~COMPRESSUS LUCASIANUS~~ *Martens.*

Haricot Beurre à cosses bleues.

= *vulgaris*

SUMMER SALAD

This recipe is a true expression of summer: delicate vegetables and leaves at the peak of their maturity. It's a very simple salad that comes straight from the garden and is tossed with a light dressing that lets its flavours sing. The Reine des Glaces is a French heritage variety and is my favourite lettuce. It is one that every gardener should grow as its growing period stretches from the beginning of spring right up to late autumn. Reine des Glaces is one of the first I enjoyed as a child and really says 'home' to me. Its flavour profile is wonderfully complex and it has a lovely crisp texture.

SERVES 4

Preparation time: 10 minutes
Cooking time: 5 minutes

For the lemon vinaigrette
200ml extra virgin olive oil
6 tbsp lemon juice
3 tbsp white wine vinegar
6 tbsp warm water
2 tsp Manuka honey
large pinch rock salt
large pinch ground white
    pepper

For the salad
100g shelled broad beans
16 breakfast radishes, with their
    leaves, sliced 2mm thick
4 baby courgettes, sliced
    lengthways 2mm thick
4 courgette flowers, torn into
    petals, stigma removed
1 young head Seurat lettuce, leaves
    separated
1 young head Reine des Glaces
    lettuce, outer leaves discarded,
    leaves separated
8 pea shoots
10g chives, cut into 2cm batons
100g goat's curd
30g heather honey honeycomb

For the lemon vinaigrette, in a medium bowl, whisk all the ingredients together. Taste and adjust the seasoning if necessary. Transfer to a bottle and shake before using to re-emulsify the dressing.

Prepare the salad. If the broad beans are very young, leave their skins on; if older blanch them for 30 seconds in plenty of boiling water, remove, refresh and pop them out of their skins.

In a large bowl, dress the broad beans, radishes, courgettes and courgette flowers in 2 tablespoons of the lemon vinaigrette. Add the lettuce leaves, radish leaves, pea shoots and chives, another 2 tablespoons of the dressing and lightly toss the salad using your fingers. Taste and correct the seasoning.

To serve, place a mound of the salad in the centre of each plate then scatter the goat's curd and honeycomb on top.

Chef's notes
Using warm water in the dressing will help to bind it.

The dressing makes more than you need but it can be stored in the fridge for up to 1 week.

Variation
Any fresh local goat's cheese, buffalo mozzarella or burrata would be delicious in place of the goat's curd.

BRUNO LOUBET'S BEAN AND VEGETABLE CHILLI

The list of ingredients here may look long and daunting but I promise you, the recipe is very simple – a one-pot wonder. This recipe was kindly given to me by a great chef – Bruno Loubet – who worked with me for many years. The strange thing is that Bruno is at heart a dedicated carnivore and has been his whole life. He comes from the south-west of France where foie gras is eaten for breakfast! – yet, miracle – he has become a very vegetable-oriented chef. His fabulous grain- and vegetable-centric London restaurant relegates meat to a supporting role, and is testimony to his skills and creativity as a chef.

Risking Bruno's wrath, I have taken a few of the original ingredients out of his vegetarian take on a chilli con carne, and have added an unusual one – 100 per cent cocoa chocolate. Chocolate is widely used in South American cooking to flavour and enrich savoury dishes and I guarantee you it really works – it belongs here. I hope he will forgive my boldness and see the wisdom of an older man. At its heart, this is a great dish: a wonderful bowl of health that delivers a meaty heartiness without a single piece of 'carne'. Thank you Bruno.

SERVES 6–8

Preparation time: 20 minutes
Cooking time: 30 minutes

For the toasted spices
1½ tsp ground coriander
1½ tsp ground cumin
2 tsp sweet smoked paprika

For the vegetable base
125g onion (about ½), cut into chunks
3 garlic cloves, crushed
125g celery, cut into 3cm chunks
70g fennel, cut into 3cm chunks
1 large carrot, peeled and cut into 3cm chunks
375g button mushrooms
1 red chilli
12g fresh ginger, peeled and finely grated or sliced
1 red pepper, cut into large dice

For the chilli
100ml rapeseed oil
large pinch sea salt

Toast the spices in a dry frying pan on a low–medium heat for 1 minute – ensure that you don't burn them; you just want to extract the essential oils.

For the vegetable base, place the onion, garlic, celery, fennel, carrot, mushrooms, chilli, ginger and red pepper in a food processor and pulse in 3-second bursts for 30 seconds, until you have 2–3mm dice. These ground vegetables will create the flavour and texture in the dish. This may need to be done in two batches depending on the capacity of your food processor bowl.

To cook the chilli, in a large saucepan on a medium heat, sweat the vegetable base in the oil with the toasted spices and a large pinch of salt for 10 minutes.

Continued overleaf →

For the flageolet beans
550ml water
100g flageolet beans

To finish the chilli
100g tomato purée
200g piquillo peppers
1 x 400g tin chopped tomatoes
1 x 240g tin red kidney beans
100g brown sauce
2 tbsp Worcestershire sauce

For the rice
260g brown basmati rice
1 bay leaf

To finish
40g chocolate (100 per cent cocoa
    solids), finely grated
10g coriander leaves, roughly
    chopped

For the flageolet beans, in a separate large saucepan on a high heat, bring the water to a boil and cook the flageolet beans for 10 minutes on a full boil until just tender. Lift the beans from the pan with a slotted spoon but keep the cooking liquor on the heat as you will use it to cook the rice.

To finish the chilli, add the tomato purée, piquillo peppers and tinned tomatoes and simmer for 10 minutes. add the kidney beans, cooked flageolet beans, brown and Worcestershire sauces and leave to cook for a further 5 minutes.

While the chilli is cooking, cook the brown rice in the broad bean cooking liquor with the bay leaf and simmer for 15–20 minutes, covered with a lid. Depending on the variety of rice, it may take a few more minutes. Once cooked drain off any excess liquid and transfer to a serving dish.

To finish, stir in the grated chocolate. Taste and adjust the seasoning as required. Serve the chilli with the chopped coriander and the brown rice alongside.

Chef's note
Brown basmati rice will have more fibre and flavour than white.

CARROTS

EVERY YEAR IN BRITAIN we eat our way through some 700,000 tons of carrots. And we are so used to seeing them on the shelves of supermarkets 52 weeks of the year that it is easy to forget that carrots are naturally a seasonal vegetable, harvested from around June to November, according to variety. After that they can be stored until around May, leaving only a few months of importing carrots from warmer climates to satisfy demand until the new season's crop arrives.

Opposite: Carrots in shades of purple, red and yellow were known long before the ubiquitous orange version took over the market from the sixteenth and seventeenth centuries onwards.

The history of carrots is complicated, not entirely clear, and the subject of numerous scholastic studies. Broadly speaking, it is generally accepted that the first cultivated carrots were grown in Afghanistan in around AD7 and were a dark purple colour, with yellow varieties appearing soon afterwards.

Carrots in various shades of purpley-red and yellow spread throughout Europe during the Middle Ages, when, it seems, the yellow colour began to predominate, possibly because the purple carrots released their dark colour during cooking, and were likely to stain cooking pots.

It was in Holland, during the sixteenth and seventeenth centuries, that the ubiquitous orange carrot, fatter than its more spindly predecessors, was developed – though the popular idea that it was bred in order to honour William of Orange (later to become William III of England) is most likely a myth!

Until recently, the orange carrot was virtually all that was grown commercially in Britain, with the focus predominantly on appearance, resistance to disease and shelf life over flavour. As a result, a whole generation has grown up with the bland taste of the average supermarket specimen, never knowing the zing and sweetness of a local or heritage variety. Fortunately, the rise and rise of the farmers' market and the weekly vegetable box has done wonders for this much maligned vegetable, re-acquainting us with the joy of bunches of imperfectly-shaped carrots, still covered in earth, their feathery green fronds still attached. And as the clamour for more interesting local and traditional varieties builds, we are seeing the re-emergence of rainbow-coloured carrots that mirror the historical shades of purple, red and yellow.

The varieties grown at Kew include the red-and-violet-skinned Rouge Sang Violette; the Spanish Black, with its purple-ish black surface and white and purple interior; and the rare Purple Afghan – the seeds of which were sent to the Heritage Seed Library in 1978 by a UN worker who found them in Afghanistan. Raymond's favourite carrot for flavour and texture, however, is Early Nantes, a nineteenth-century orange heritage variety.

*Left: The statue of
'A Sower' captures
the spirit of the Kew
garden in which
heritage and often
rare seeds of carrots
and other vegetables
and fruits have grown
and flourished to
delight visitors.*

The various colours of carrots are not only ornamental, but each contributes a different health-giving property. Orange carrots contain high levels of beta-carotene, a pigment that the body converts into vitamin A. Although the old adage that carrots help you see in the dark isn't strictly true, vitamin A is important for eye health and the immune system. Purple carrots contain anthocyanins, which may help reduce the risk of some diseases, while red carrots contain the antioxidant lycopene.

Wild carrots – as distinct from the cultivated vegetable – were known as far back as Greek and Roman times. Often a pale creamy-white in colour, they were frequently confused with their close relation, the parsnip, which further complicates the whole carrot history. However, it is clear from ancient botanical manuscripts that wild carrots were considered more of a medicine than a food. Logged in the archives at Kew is a copy of one of the world's earliest herbals, *De Materia Medica*. Written by the physician Pedanius Dioscorides, he details some 600 plants and their medicinal uses, gleaned from his travels as a physician in the Roman army during the time of Emperor Nero in the first century AD. Born in Anazarbus near Tarsus, in what is present day Turkey, he wrote the original manuscript, *Perì üles iatrichès*, in Greek, but it was swiftly translated into Latin, and later Arabic and other languages. Dioscorides focused on the medicinal aspect of carrot seeds and leaves in potions that were variously seen as a diuretic, an aphrodisiac, an aid to conception (or an inducement of miscarriage) and a remedy for bites and stings.

Interestingly, a later Byzantine illustrated version of the herbal, dating from AD512, shows the carrot as being orange coloured – so in an additional twist in the complex tale of the carrot, it is possible that the colour we are familiar with today was actually in existence long before its more obvious commercial emergence in sixteenth-century Holland.

Right: An ancient depiction of a carrot, from the facsimile edition of Dioscorides' De Materia Medica *(*Codex Vindobonensis med. Gr. 1 der Österreichischen Nationalbibliothek, 1965–70) in the National Library of Austria in Vienna.*

اِستافلِنوس اَعرِبي

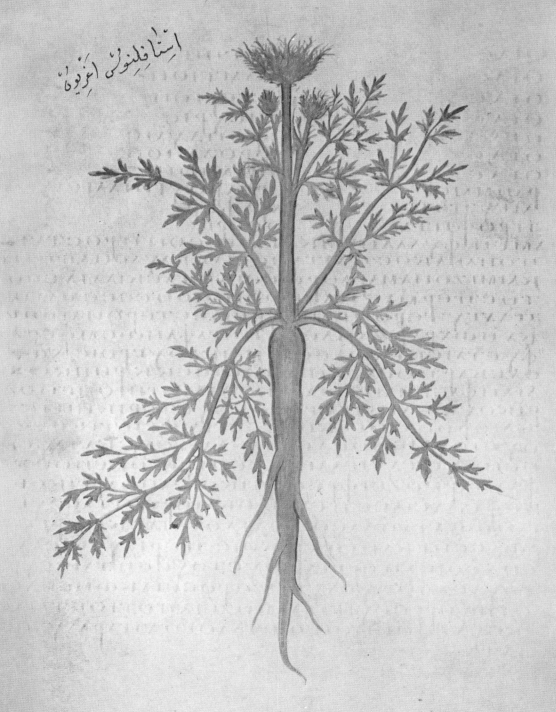

GROWING NOTES

Prepare your beds by digging in some well-rotted compost the autumn before sowing.

Sow seeds directly into the soil between March and July depending on the variety.

Make sure you remove any stones from the bed. If the developing roots (the carrots) hit one of these, they can 'fork', i.e. split, in order to go around the stone.

Sow the seeds in shallow drills (narrow furrows) – you can make these by laying a broom handle along the soil and pressing down. The drills only need to be about 1cm deep.

Sprinkle the seed thinly along the length of the drill – if you sow thickly it will make harder work of thinning out the seedlings as they grow. Cover with soil and water well.

Carrots, especially smaller varieties, such as Chantenay, also grow well in containers on a patio. Choose pots that are at least 20cm deep, plant in compost, supplement with a liquid feed throughout the growing season and make sure the compost doesn't dry out.

If growing in beds, make sure the soil stays moist until the seeds begin to germinate and produce seedlings – this will take around 10–20 days. Keep weed free so that the seedlings don't get crowded out.

At this stage you can thin them out to about one seedling every 2–4cm. Don't take out any more; you want to leave as many in as possible at this stage, in case of pest damage.

After another four weeks or so you can thin them out again to a spacing of about 10cm.

The main pest is carrot fly. 'If the female flies have a whiff of carrots, they home in and lay their eggs on top of the soil. When they hatch, the larvae burrow down and into the carrots,' says Alice, who, before sowing, surrounded the beds with very fine carrot fly netting, 60–90cm high, to keep out the pests. 'They fly quite low,' she says, 'so there is no need for it to be higher.'

Try to avoid crushing the foliage as you thin the seedlings, and don't leave any that you pull up lying on the soil as it is that freshly-released carrot aroma that the flies can't resist.

The Kew gardeners have also tried some companion planting – putting in a crop of spring onions alongside the carrots. 'Companion planting can have an effect in various ways,' says Alice. 'Sometimes you might put in a sacrificial plant, i.e. one which a certain pest will go for first, limiting damage to your preferred crop. Or it can work by confusing the pest with a strong competitive smell – in this case the onions may douse down the attractive smell of the carrots.'

Some carrot varieties, such as the obviously named Resistafly, have been bred to be more resistant to the pests, so if carrot fly is a persistent problem it may be worth trying these.

Throughout the growing season you only need to water if the soil becomes dry.

Harvest early varieties, such as Early Nantes, around nine weeks after sowing, and maincrop varieties after around 12–16 weeks. Obviously this is dependent on the weather, so pull up a test carrot first. As soon as the carrot is big enough to eat, it is ready – size is really a matter of personal preference and variety. Just don't let them get too large or you will sacrifice flavour and the carrots will be more woody. Lift carefully, using a fork if the soil is heavy.

RAYMOND'S FLAVOUR NOTES

The variety that I really love is the Early Nantes, which in our taste tests won out over every other variety. My parents grew it and at Kew it also found its earth. I associate it with that wonderful, fresh, intense, 'true' carrot flavour. The Chantenay carrot can also be lovely, but it is a designer carrot, sweet, fast-growing and quite resistant to disease.

When I was growing up, in 90 per cent of French houses, families would eat crudités before the main meal every Sunday, and in ours the carrot would always be the star. It was a cheap, nutritious way to feed seven of us and we loved it. My mum would grate the carrots very, very finely to extract the juices, which she would mix with olive oil and lemon juice and a pinch of salt for the dressing. It was so tasty and healthy. The carrots would be in a big dish in the middle of the table, surrounded by tomatoes, boiled egg, cucumber and grated celeriac in mayonnaise... Wonderful.

Ten years ago I had a big battle to win against the young chefs in my kitchen, to make them understand that a baby carrot, like a baby courgette, is very pretty, but does it have real flavour? No, because it needs to mature. There is a flavour curve in the life of many fruits and vegetables that traces their development of sugar and therefore their taste. In the case of the carrot this is demonstrated very well. At the beginning, when the carrot is a baby, it tastes of very little, then the flavour curve arcs upwards as more sugars develop, until it reaches its peak, when the carrot is a medium size – adolescent, if you like – and its sweetness is balanced with a vegetal complexity. Then, as the carrot matures and becomes more coarse and fibrous, the flavour curve arcs downwards again, as the sugars become more dominant and detrimental to the flavour, to the point where all you are tasting is sweetness.

CARROT, CUMIN AND BARLEY SUMMER STEW

For many years I've had a deep longing to create a form of risotto using barley, but as the Italians might tell me off, I decided to play safe and call this a stew. The spices add the complex notes – the heat should be gentle not overpowering. The dish is wholesome, satisfying and healthy yet luxuriously creamy and a fantastic showcase for the big flavour of my favourite Early Nantes carrots.

SERVES 4

Preparation time: 15 minutes
Cooking time: 1 hour 30 minutes

For the carrots
500ml carrot juice
100ml water
large pinch of sea salt
1 tsp ground cumin
6 carrots (ideally Early Nantes),
    skin on, scrubbed, halved
    lengthways then cut into
    1cm slices at an angle

For the barley
2 tbsp rapeseed oil
80g white onion (about
    ½ medium), chopped
2 Passilla Bajio chillies,
    deseeded and finely chopped
150g pearl barley
1 tsp ground cumin
1 corn cob, cooked in boiling water
    for 20 minutes, covered
4 rainbow chard leaves, rolled
    and chopped; stems cut
    into 3cm pieces
3 spring onions, finely sliced
a small bunch coriander, chopped
juice of ½ lemon

To finish
1½ tbsp rapeseed oil
micro coriander (optional)

For the carrots, in a large saucepan on a medium heat, bring the carrot juice and water to the boil, then add the salt and cumin. Add the carrots and simmer gently for 10 minutes until they are cooked through. Remove from the heat, scoop out the carrots and reserve the cooking liquor.

To cook the barley, in a medium saucepan on a medium heat, add the oil and sweat the onions and chilli for 5 minutes, covered with a lid, until softened. Stir in the barley and cumin and continue to sweat for 1 minute. Add 500ml of the carrot cooking liquor to the pan, bring to a gentle simmer, then cover with a lid and cook for 50–55 minutes, stirring from time to time, until the barley swells and is firm with a good bite. Check the texture, taste and check the seasoning, and cook for a few minutes more, if necessary. Set aside in the pan.

To finish the barley risotto, using a long knife, carefully cut the kernels off the corn cob by running a knife along the central core. Keep four of the biggest lengths intact to use as garnish. Set these aside then release the kernels from the rest. Add the chard stems and leaves, spring onions and loose corn kernels to the barley pan and stir, then place the pan back on a medium heat and cook for 12 minutes. Add the coriander and cook for 1 minute until wilted. Finally, taste and adjust the seasoning if required, then add the lemon juice to sharpen the flavour.

To finish, in a medium frying pan on a medium heat, fry the cooked carrot pieces in the rapeseed oil for 6–7 minutes, until caramelised. Add the reserved pieces of sliced corn to the pan and cook for 3 minutes until they begin to brown. Spoon out the caramelised carrots, add them to the barley risotto and divide the risotto evenly between four plates. Finish with a length of sliced corn and micro coriander, if using. Serve immediately.

CARROT CAKE

Carrot cake history cannot be traced to a single nation. What is certain, however, is that carrots have been used as a natural sweetener since the Middle Ages, when they were put into puddings. As a Frenchman, I confess that I have always regarded the British tendency to use vegetables in cakes with a degree of scepticism, but I was pleasantly surprised with the result. The French would probably use butter whereas my British friends would most likely use oil, which will keep the cake moist for longer. The spicing and flavouring of the cake is up to you: make it your canvas with a hint of cumin, allspice or cardamom as well as, or in place of, the cinnamon and ginger, and even add orange zest if you wish.

Although this recipe makes two cakes, it freezes very well (un-iced) and can be kept frozen for up to 1 month. Ice the cake once it is thoroughly defrosted.

MAKES 2 LOAVES

Preparation time: 15 minutes
Cooking time: 45 minutes

For the carrot cake
300g light brown sugar
3 medium eggs
100g marzipan
1 tsp Vanilla Purée (see page 281)
    or good-quality vanilla extract
300ml sunflower oil
300g plain flour, sifted
1 tsp bicarbonate of soda
1 tsp baking powder
½ tsp sea salt
1 tsp ground cinnamon
1 tsp ground ginger
100g sultanas
300g carrots, grated

For the icing and topping (optional)
75g cream cheese
25g unsalted butter, softened
75g icing sugar
30g pecan nuts/walnuts, toasted,
    to decorate

Preheat the oven to 170°C/Gas Mark 3½. Line two 26 x 9 x 8cm terrine moulds or 900g loaf tins with baking parchment leaving an overhang of paper.

Prepare the cake batter. In a food mixer on a medium speed, whisk together the sugar, eggs, marzipan and vanilla purée or extract for about 4 minutes, until smooth and light. Continue mixing and pour in the sunflower oil in a steady stream.

Mix together the flour, bicarbonate of soda, baking powder, salt and spices and sift. Fold into the wet mixture until fully incorporated. Lastly, fold in the sultanas and carrot, then pour the mixture into your lined terrine moulds or tins.

Bake the carrot cakes in the oven for 45 minutes. To check if the cakes are cooked, insert a sharp paring knife into each and touch it to your lips; it should feel hot. For greater accuracy, insert a probe into the centre of the cake – it will read 76–82°C. At this temperature all the ingredients will be cooked through. Remove the cakes from the oven, take them out of the moulds and leave to cool on a cooling rack. It is important to turn them out of their moulds immediately so that they don't steam inside the moulds. Of course, the cake can be eaten just as it is, but for more of a celebration, ice it.

To make the icing, briskly beat the cream cheese, butter and icing sugar together in a large mixing bowl. Once the cakes are completely cool, use a palette knife to spread the icing on top of each loaf and finish by scattering over a few whole toasted pecan nuts or walnuts.

99·

CAROTTE.

Left: Carrot (Daucus carota) *from the nineteenth-century herbal,* Flore Medicale *(vol 2., plate 99) by the French physician and botanist, François-Pierre Chaumeton (1775–1819). The illustration is by Pierre Jean François Turpin, one of the leading French botanical painters of the time.*

GARLIC

'AS A FRENCHMAN, garlic is synonymous with my country and my whole identity. What makes me happy is that this wonderful food that was once so alien to the British palate has now been completely embraced to the point where my British friends eat as much as me,' says Raymond. I can't say enough about what a wonderful nutritional powerhouse garlic is – and a complete medicine cabinet. Everybody should eat a clove a day – and an apple, too, of course – preferably afterwards, if you want to keep your friends!'

Hailed as a protector against vampires, revered by the ancient Greeks and Egyptians, garlic is a nutritional powerhouse of flavour and goodness.

Legendary as a protector against vampires, garlic was revered by the ancient Greeks and Egyptians for its medicinal properties. It was used in mummification and often buried with Egyptian corpses in their tombs. By the time the pyramids at Giza were being built, around 680,000 kilos of garlic were apparently being brought in to keep the workers going, and when drought limited the supplies they responded by going on strike!

Today garlic is hailed as an antiseptic and an antioxidant, helping to protect against free radicals which can cause damage to cells and encourage cancers; and it is also linked with improved blood circulation, healthier cholesterol levels and the lowering of blood pressure.

In the kitchen garlic can be enjoyed in two phases: 'new season', more often called 'green' or 'wet' garlic; and 'dried' garlic, which is the familiar form we see in shops and supermarkets. New season garlic is lifted from the ground around May, before the bulb has properly formed into individual cloves. 'It is juicy, mild, sweet and delicate, yet with the zing of the garlic flavour we know, and you can eat the whole of the plant,' says Raymond. 'Chop it all up and put it into a salad, sweat it as the base of a risotto, add it to scrambled eggs or stir-fry it.'

By June or July, depending on the variety, the bulb will have formed individual cloves whose skin has toughened enough to need peeling, and the flavour will have intensified. These bulbs, once lifted, are allowed to dry out and can be kept for up to around nine months.

There are two kinds of garlic: softneck and hardneck. Softneck varieties form several rings of cloves with larger ones on the outside and smaller ones in the centre. These are the variety that supermarkets prefer, as they keep better and for longer.

Hardneck varieties are distinguished by their curling green stems, known as scapes, which can be taken off in June (before they have a chance to flower). These have a mild flavour and can be eaten raw or cooked, in the same way as new season garlic. Although the bulbs tend to produce fewer larger cloves around the central stalk, and don't keep as well as softneck varieties, they often have a richer, more interesting and complex flavour.

Tab.109.

Allium sativum. L.

These days 70 per cent of British garlic comes from the Isle of Wight. According to Colin Boswell, whose family run The Garlic Farm on the island, garlic was most likely grown on the island in Roman times. However it only took off during the Second World War, when a flotilla of Free French motor torpedo boats was stationed at Cowes. The crews used to frequent the Painters Arms pub, whose landlord, Bill Spidy, had a small farm next door to the site of the current Garlic Farm.

The sailors, complaining about the blandness of the pub food, asked the landlord if he would grow some garlic for them. He didn't have any to start off the crop, but two RAF friends who were seconded to Special Operations, flying agents in and out of occupied France, helped out. On 27th October 1942, a Lysander aircraft piloted by one Officer Bridger landed two agents in the fields in the Auvergne region and then loaded a sack of garlic from a local farmer which he brought back to Billy Spidy, who duly planted it, keeping the Frenchmen happy for the duration of the war.

The varieties chosen for the garden at Kew are all grown on the Isle of Wight – although all originate in France. Of the hardneck varieties, Lautrec Wight, originally from Toulouse in the south-west of France, is white-skinned with pink cloves; Carcassonne Wight is another exceptional pink-cloved garlic; while the softneck varieties include Picardy Wight, originally from the Somme in Normandy, where the bulbs are plaited and smoked. Slow growing, it is also one of the longest-keeping varieties. If harvested after mid-July it will keep until around the following March/April. The final softneck variety, Early Purple Wight comes from south-west France, but is raised from ancient Chinese stock. It has large purple bulbs and as its name suggests, it is one of the earliest garlics, which tends to be eaten soon after harvesting, rather than being allowed to dry.

'The first that we tasted, the Picardy Wight, had all the characteristics that the French love,' says Raymond. 'It was fragrant and juicy, but it was so incredibly powerful, it exploded in the mouth. I couldn't believe the strength of a single clove. Of course, to show everyone how much I love garlic, I bit into a huge chunk of it and I suffered! So I would say, you only need to use a little bit of the Picardy Wight. The garlic that was the best was the hardneck Lautrec Wight: less intense than the Picardy Wight, but with a lovely flavour, so a good all-rounder in the kitchen.'

Left: Garlic (Allium sativum) *as depicted by Austrian artist Ignaz Stenzel in Daniel Wagner's* Pharmaceutisch-medicinische Botanik, *vol. I: t.109, published in Vienna in 1828.*

GROWING NOTES

Although in theory you could just plant garlic bought in the shops or supermarket, it is best to buy from a garden centre, so that you know you are buying certified disease-free stock that is suited to the British climate.

While garlic is sold for either spring or autumn planting, you will usually get the fattest crop if you plant in November.

Sow straight into the ground. There is nothing to be gained from starting garlic indoors or in a greenhouse as the cloves need a period of cold to induce them to split and build into a bulb.

Garlic prefers a light, free-draining soil and sun. Dig in some well-rotted manure or compost at least 3–4 weeks before planting.

To plant, break the garlic bulb of your choice gently into cloves, taking care not to damage them. If there is a wound or bruising, the clove

will be more susceptible to picking up a soil-borne infection and then rotting. As soon as you have broken the bulb into cloves, make a small hole just big enough for each clove to sit 2.5cm below the surface of the soil – space them about 15cm apart. Put the clove in, root-side down and tip upwards, and cover with 2.5cm of soil.

If you have a patio garden, you can grow garlic in pots, typically three in a 15cm pot, six in a 20cm pot and eight to ten in a 25cm pot, spaced evenly. Make sure you don't let the compost dry out.

On a plot, plant in rows, leaving about 30cm between each row. Don't crowd the plants as this increases humidity and the likelihood of any leek rust (see opposite) spreading.

Cover with a net or garden fleece until the leaves appear, to stop birds pulling up the cloves.

Right and opposite: Hardneck varieties of garlic (see page 112) produce flower stems or 'scapes' around June, which need to be snapped off. Don't waste them, as they have a lovely delicate flavour, which will perk up salads, scrambled eggs or stir-fries.

Keep weed free and only water during dry spells, making sure you stop watering around two weeks before the anticipated harvest time, as too much water can cause rotting.

With hardneck varieties, snap off the flower stems or scapes, which appear around June, even if you are not going to use them in salads or cooking, so that the plant can focus all of its energy into producing the bulb underground.

The two main enemies of garlic are onion white rot and leek rust. Onion white rot is a persistent fungus that usually occurs when any of the allium family – garlic, onions, leeks – have been continuously grown in the same area of the garden. The sign of onion white rot is that the leaves turn yellow and wilt, or if the ground is wet, they become loose in the soil. If you lift the garlic, you will see a white, furry, fungal growth around the bulbs, dotted with tiny black globules resembling poppy seeds. Unfortunately, there is no remedy for onion white rot; the only

solution is to pull up the affected garlics and destroy them. When the rest of the crop has been harvested – assuming it hasn't all been affected, then don't grow any more alliums in the same spot for at least eight years.

Leek rust is a fungal disease that shows itself as small orange blisters on leaves from May onwards. At The Garlic Farm they have a novel idea for controlling early signs of leek rust: painting the blisters with alcohol – apparently cheap gin will do! 'A mild attack usually won't affect your crop, especially if it is late on,' advises Alice. 'If it takes hold earlier, however, the leaves can shrivel, and since their job is to photosynthesise and create energy for the bulb to swell, the garlic won't plump up as well.' Again, pull up and destroy any affected bulbs, and when the crop is harvested avoid planting alliums in the same spot for three years.

Onion fly can also be a problem. The fly lays its eggs close to or on the plant, and when the eggs

Four varieties of garlic flourishing in the light, free-draining soil of the garden at Kew.

hatch, maggots form which can bore into the garlic bulb and cause it to collapse. If a plant dies back around May, lift it – you will probably see a fat maggot inside the bulb – and destroy it, to stop it from pupating in the soil. Keeping the growing area weed free offers some protection, as can covering plants with horticultural fleece.

If you want to use some of the crop as 'new season' or 'wet' garlic, lift it around May, while the leaves are still green, and the bulb will be swollen, but not formed into individual cloves.

By around the end of June/early July (depending on the variety), November-planted garlic will be fully formed, more pungent and ready for harvesting and drying (varieties planted in spring will be ready a little later).

The bulbs are ready to be lifted when almost all of the leaves have turned yellow – often at

this point the plants will also go 'weak at the knees', i.e. the leaves will just fold over.

Lift the garlic carefully, using a hand fork, being careful not to pierce any part of the bulb, as this will affect its ability to keep well. Then, leaving the leaves still on, either tie in bunches of about six bulbs or lay them in wooden trays somewhere airy to dry out until the skin is 'rustling dry' – this drying process will take about three weeks.

'If you were to weigh a freshly harvested garlic bulb, it would probably be around 10–12 grams,' says Raymond. 'When it has dried, it will weigh about half that, as the moisture has evaporated. As it becomes drier, the flavour becomes more concentrated and pungent and the skin becomes like fine paper, which is easier to peel.'

RAYMOND'S FLAVOUR NOTES

Even I was amazed at the different strengths of flavour in our garlic taste tests (see page 115).

Forget about taking out the green germ that you sometimes see at the heart of a clove of garlic – that is its life force, ready to shoot, which is saying, 'I want to go back into the earth and produce baby garlics.' Recipes sometimes tell you to remove it because it is bitter. I think that is nonsense; I've been eating every part of the clove all my life!

If I am going to sweat some garlic in oil with onions for the base of a dish, I will just chop it, because it will soften and diffuse its flavours. However, if it is being added raw at the end of a dish, for example in a *persillade* (see page 32), then I would prefer to grind the garlic to a smooth paste, which takes a big strong knife and a firm wrist to work the flat of the knife against the chopped cloves. There are also some good presses, if you prefer. If you are not using chopped or crushed garlic straight away, cover it with cling film – if it is exposed to air it can discolour.

Garlic is one of the sweetest vegetables, so if you want to sauté chopped garlic and onion, put in the garlic after the onions have been cooking for a few minutes as its high sugar concentration would otherwise cause it to brown before the onions, and if it starts to burn it can become bitter.

If you roast the cloves whole in the oven, they become incredibly sweet and meltingly soft. A chicken roasted with 40–60 cloves of garlic around it is a beautiful thing.

Right: Garlic is one of the sweetest vegetables, and whole heads of it will become meltingly tender and even sweeter when broken into cloves and roasted in the oven.

BALSAMIC GLAZED-GARLIC, SUMMER TOMATOES AND ROAST CHICKEN LEGS

For this simple dish to be successful, the tomatoes need to be extremely ripe to deliver the right taste, colour, texture and plenty of juice. You can use cherry tomatoes, which will create a sweeter dish, but I've found that San Marzano or Roma tomatoes have been designed to make the perfect sauce. Their high ratio of flesh to juice means that they have the perfect balance between the two, more sugar and less acidity, and they will cook down to the texture you need here.

This recipe is based on an infamous French garlic dish, much loved by the nation: chicken roasted with 40 garlic cloves. I have been kind to you and have reduced the number to 20. Although this still sounds like a lot, you will find that the cloves, once cooked, lose their aggressiveness and potency and become wonderfully sweet. They also retain all their nutritional properties (see page 112).

SERVES 4

Preparation time: 20 minutes
Cooking time: 1 hour

For the chicken and balsamic-glazed garlic

4 organic or free-range
    chicken legs, cut into leg and
    thigh
2 tbsp rapeseed oil
20 garlic cloves, peeled but
    left whole
1 thyme sprig
1 oregano sprig
2 tbsp 8-year-old balsamic vinegar,
sea salt and freshly ground
    black pepper

For the tomatoes

100g white onion
    (about ½), sliced
4 tbsp olive oil
150g fennel, cut into 1cm dice
1 tarragon sprig, chopped
600g San Marzano tomatoes,
    roughly chopped
6 coriander sprigs, roughly
    chopped

Preheat the oven to 150°C/Gas Mark 2.

For the chicken, season the legs and thighs evenly with salt and pepper. In a large, ovenproof sauté pan on a medium–high heat, add the oil and fry the chicken pieces, skin-side down, for 8–10 minutes, covered with a lid, until golden brown. Turn the pieces over, add the garlic, thyme and oregano and transfer to the oven to roast for 30 minutes.

Using a slotted spoon, transfer the chicken legs and thighs to a tray, cover with foil and keep in a warm place. Leaving the garlic in the pan, spoon out the excess fat and deglaze the pan with the balsamic vinegar and 1 tablespoon of water, scraping any browned bits from the bottom with a wooden spoon. Cook for a further minute until the balsamic vinegar reduces and becomes sticky. Pour the juices and garlic over the chicken and set aside.

For the tomatoes, in a large sauté pan on a medium heat, sweat the onion in the oil for 3 minutes, then add the fennel and sweat for 3 minutes with the tarragon and two pinches of salt and pepper, covering the pan with a lid. Add the tomatoes and cook for a further 15 minutes, covered with a lid; the tomatoes will break down and create a beautiful sauce. Add the coriander, taste and adjust the seasoning if required.

To serve, divide the tomatoes between four large plates or bowls, arrange a leg and thigh on top, divide the glazed garlic between the plates or bowls and spoon the balsamic glaze and any roasting juices over and around the chicken.

SMOKED GARLIC FOCACCIA

Living in Britain has enriched me enormously – its multicultural backdrop has influenced every part of me: my food, my ideas, my creativity – and this recipe is testimony to that mixing of cultures. I've allied my national beloved bulb of fragrance and Frenchness with an Italian classic as homage to a bread that I ate in Italy, one of the greatest I tasted in my life – it was pure delight: rustic and topped with caramelised garlic cooked in balsamic vinegar.

Making focaccia is a brilliant, easy way of getting into bread-making and mastering the mysteries of yeast, which of course creates the magic of the fermentation within the bread. This hearty, simple version of focaccia has an unusual smokey tang. You can buy smoked garlic in specialised shops and online or you can buy a small smoker and do it yourself at home!

MAKES 2 LOAVES

Preparation time: 10 minutes;
    plus proving
Cooking time: 15 minutes

For the dough
unsalted butter, for greasing
500g strong white organic bread
    flour, plus a little extra for
    dusting
4 tsp sea salt
2 rosemary sprigs, finely chopped
10 smoked garlic cloves,
    finely chopped
15g fresh yeast
280ml water
6–7 tbsp good-quality olive
    oil

Lightly grease two round 20cm x 3cm baking tins, then dust them with flour. If you do not have round tins, shape and press the whole dough into a roasting tin or deep baking tray to make one large focaccia or simply shape it roughly with your hands on a baking tray.

To prepare the dough, in a large mixing bowl, mix the flour, 2 teaspoons of the salt, the rosemary and garlic. In a separate bowl dissolve the yeast in the water.

Make a well in the middle of the flour, add the yeast mixture, half the oil and gradually mix together with your fingertips. Once the dough comes together, start to knead on a lightly floured work surface for 3–4 minutes. This will work the gluten and give the bread dough its strength and structure. Add the remaining oil whilst kneading and continue for a further 5–8 minutes. Of course, this can be done by a machine – it's easier but you won't derive as much pleasure as doing it by hand. Place the dough back into the bowl, cover with a clean cloth and prove at room temperature for 30 minutes.

Divide the dough in half and roll each piece out to fit into one of the tins. Press the dough down with your fingertips to cover the base. Prove in a warm place (at 30°C maximum), again covered with a clean cloth until it doubles in volume; this usually takes 30–40 minutes. It's important to cover the bread with a cloth, as it will exclude any draft and prevent a crust forming.

Continued overleaf $\rightarrow$

To bake
good-quality olive oil, for brushing
2 tsp sea salt

Preheat the oven to 270°C/Gas Mark 9.

To bake, lightly brush the dough with a little olive oil and sprinkle the sea salt or other garnishes (see below) over the top. Bake in the oven for 12–15 minutes or until golden and crisp. Turn out of the tins to cool on a wire rack. It's important not to leave the bread in the tin, otherwise it will steam and the crust will not be as crisp.

Chef's notes
Yeast hates salt. Salt will dehydrate the yeast and prevent it from activating so your bread will not rise. Make sure you follow the instructions carefully and mix the dough as directed.

You can also add a selection of toppings to this bread, such as pesto, sun-blushed tomatoes, herbs, olives and caramelised onion. Just scatter them on top prior to baking.

You could also use fresh or dried garlic in place of the smoked garlic. At Kew I have grown four varieties of garlic, including the Carcassonne Wight, Picardy Wight and the Early Purple Wight. But it was the wonderful Lautrec Wight, a variety originally from France but grown on the Isle of Wight for many years, that I found to be the most flavoursome.

GOOSEBERRIES

WHAT

A STRANGE AND SPLENDID PLANT is the gooseberry bush; fierce thorns guarding its clusters of taut little orbs, their ethereal, veined skins looking fit to burst in an explosion of exquisite, complex sourness. If ever there was a truly British fruit it is the gooseberry, which has been grown in gardens in this country since the thirteenth century.

Isabella Beeton reflected the Victorian love of gooseberries, as exemplified by Kew's director of the time, Joseph Hooker. Mrs Beeton observed that the skill of the English gardener had brought the fruit to a 'high state of perfection'.

The Victorians adored the gooseberry – at least until it found a rival in the newly fashionable rhubarb (see page 41) – and they cultivated both 'cooking' varieties and sweeter 'dessert' varieties. They made wine with gooseberries, baked them in tarts and transformed them into a sauce for serving with mackerel. In her *Book of Household Management* Mrs Beeton wrote of the gooseberry that, 'the high state of perfection to which it has been here brought, is due to the skill of the English gardeners,' noting, 'Malic and citric acid blended with sugar, produce the pleasant flavour of the gooseberry; and upon the proper development of these properties depends the success of all cooking operations with which they are connected.'

The growing of gooseberries was one of the many shared interests between Charles Darwin, who cultivated some 54 varieties at his family home, Down House, and his lifelong friend Joseph Hooker, director of Kew between 1865 and 1885. Joseph, who followed his father, William, in the directorship, is widely celebrated as one of the leading botanists and explorers of the Victorian era, in what was a golden age of horticultural research and discovery. Darwin's son Francis recalled in his memoir that on Joseph Hooker's visits to Down House, he would eat gooseberries in the kitchen garden with the Darwin children. His keenness for the fruit and his enjoyment of turning up at Down House each gooseberry season became something of a shared joke, so that when Joseph sent some bananas to Darwin from the Kew hothouses – possibly as a thank you – the family christened them 'Kew gooseberries'.

In the north of England, particularly in Cheshire and Lancashire, and in the Midlands, gooseberry clubs sprang up, organising annual shows at which the heaviest berries won prizes. There was even a publication, *The Gooseberry Growers' Register,* which featured the results of the competitions. By 1845 there were some 171 clubs recorded, growing a huge number of different varieties, many sporting colourful, patriotic names such as Roaring Lion or Nelson's Waves.

The clubs went into decline after the First World War, but a few competitions still continue, the most famous being the Egton Bridge Show in Whitby, which has been going strong since 1800. Every year competitors

Above: Sweet Xenia gooseberries will turn to red towards the end of June; and opposite, red and yellow, as well as green gooseberries were grown centuries ago, as demonstrated in this, The Goosebury, plate IV, taken from Pomona Britannica, vol. 1–2, a series of images of fruit by the English artist George Brookshaw (1751–1823).

still bring their red, white, yellow and green berries to be weighed on an old-fashioned Victorian twin-pan scale, with cups and shields being awarded to the winners in each class, and the crowning of the overall 'Champion Berry'.

For Raymond, not only is the idea of growing fruits or vegetables for size over flavour a completely alien concept, but until the Kew project, he had never cooked a gooseberry. 'What a mystery gooseberries were to me,' he admits. 'In France they are rarely used; the only tart-tasting fruit we grew was rhubarb. Yes, I had tasted a few gooseberries in my life – picked raw, but they were sour and bitter, and you pricked your fingers on their spiteful thorns when you plucked them. It was the mistake of youth that I took no interest in them. So when it was suggested that we grow some gooseberries in the garden at Kew I had to discover everything I could about them. But I am a fast learner!'

Since so many of the old varieties have disappeared, those being grown at Kew are relatively modern. They include Invicta, which dates from the 1960s and produces almost twice as many berries as most other varieties; and the newer Hinnomaki and Captivator, both of which have red berries, and Xenia, with its pinky-red, very sweet fruit.

'What I learned was that gooseberries are in danger of losing their Britishness at a pace that is alarming,' says Raymond. The same applies to strawberries and cherries, because many of the beautiful old heritage varieties have been lost, and new hybrid varieties are being bred, not only for their resistance to disease, but for their looks and their higher sugar content. As a result many varieties of gooseberry are becoming overly sweet, quite neutral in flavour and boring, when what you want is that zing and sharpness in the mouth. 'So please, let us bring back the character of the traditional gooseberry that the Victorians loved.'

The green gooseberry
Invicta dates from
the 1960s and is
known as one of the
heaviest cropping of all
varieties.

GROWING NOTES

If you are impatient for more than a smattering of fruit in the first year, buy bare-rooted bushes that are two or three years old, or container-grown bushes, both of which can be grown on a short leg/trunk of 10–15cm. This is the shape that is favoured in the garden at Kew, as raising the bushes above the ground allows better air circulation, which in turn helps to reduce the risk of American gooseberry mildew (see opposite). If necessary, remove some of the lower branches when you plant, to emphasise this length of 'leg'.

Choose your variety carefully: some, usually red, are bred as 'dessert' gooseberries and are naturally sweet, however even the most tart green 'cooking' gooseberry will develop more sugar the longer it stays on the bush.

Bare-rooted bushes need to be planted between late autumn and spring; while bushes grown in containers can go into the ground at any time, except when it is frozen, parched or waterlogged.

If planting more than one bush, space them 1.2–1.5m apart.

Dig a hole bigger than the root ball and its spread of roots. If the bush has been grown in a container, lightly tease out the roots before positioning. Firm in with the removed soil and water well.

Mulch around the base with about 5cm of compost or fine-composted bark to help retain moisture in the soil.
Like most fruit, gooseberries attract birds, which will often eat the developing buds during the winter, and then go for the ripening fruit in the summer. Keep birds at bay by covering the bushes with fine netting or a fruit cage.

Water in dry spells, so that the soil doesn't dry out, especially when the fruits start swelling.

The main pests that affect gooseberry bushes are the gooseberry sawfly species larvae (which resemble caterpillars). These can strip the leaves of a plant before the fruit ripens. 'We have been very lucky at Kew, and have not had a problem with them,' says Alice. 'You just have to be vigilant. From mid-spring onwards check the undersides of leaves, especially towards the centre of the bush. Remove any eggs before they hatch, then burn any infected leaves (don't compost them). If you keep the bush well pruned and less dense in the centre (see opposite), there is less chance of the fly taking hold before you spot the eggs.'

American gooseberry mildew can also be a problem, even though there are now varieties bred to be more resistant to it. It shows first as powdery grey-white patches on the leaves and fruit, which then turn brown, and young shoots may become stunted and die. The best prevention is to increase the air flow throughout the branches by pruning well (see opposite).

You can start harvesting the fruit from 'cooking' varieties during late May or early June, removing about half the crop first, i.e. every other berry. This helps the bush to go on cropping for longer. By around July the remainder will have swollen and developed their natural sugars and will be tasting sweeter, so, depending on the variety, can often be eaten raw. 'Dessert' varieties are usually ready for picking from mid to late June. Be aware, though, that there is a short window before they turn from taut and sweet to mushy.

'**In winter** when the bush is dormant,' advises Joe, 'remove the three d's: dead, diseased or damaged branches. Take off any lower branches to maintain the "leg" of the bush, and any crossing branches. Prune the remaining leading

shoots by half to one third, aiming to create a goblet shaped bush.' In spring, prune again to 5–6 main stems of around 20cm to create an open framework. Cutting back new side shoots on these main stems in midsummer improves the air flow around the bush, limiting the chance of fungal problems.

RAYMOND'S FLAVOUR NOTES

Of the green varieties of gooseberry, my favourite was Invicta: old-fashioned, tart and with a hint of elderflower.

The red varieties, Hinnomaki, Captivator and Xenia, are sweeter, more gentle in flavour but still delicious.

A gooseberry needs to be firm. An over-ripe berry becomes soft like a marshmallow and almost completely sweet, so it loses most of its tartness and character.

Because I knew that gooseberries and elderflowers are a classic British combination, I began researching traditional recipes and came across a very simple one for gooseberry and elderflower jelly in the book, *Good Things*, written many years ago by my dear friend Jane Grigson – a wonderful person

who was so supportive of me and my food when I started out. She says something that I find quite fascinating. She talks about the relationship between gooseberries, Frontignan wine and elderflowers. Apparently in the eighteenth and early nineteenth centuries, which was the great period of growing and eating gooseberries in Britain, the French dessert wine Frontignan, made from muscat grapes on the Languedoc coast, was also very popular. So much so that people began making their own elderflower wine, which also had a muscat flavour and became known as English Frontignan. Jane suggests that it may have been drinking these wines with summer fruit and puddings which made people realise how perfectly the fragrance of muscat – and therefore elderflowers – goes with gooseberries. Bless her!

BRAISED PIG CHEEKS WITH STEWED GOOSEBERRIES

As a Frenchman, cooking with gooseberries has been a great experiment, but instinctively I knew their tartness would perfectly cut through the sweet unctuousness of slow-cooked pig cheeks. And I was right.

SERVES 4

Preparation time: 15 minutes, plus marinating
Cooking time: 3½ hours

For the pig cheeks
2 pig cheeks (about 450g in total)
300ml white wine
40g unsalted butter
130g onion (1 small), chopped
110g carrot, peeled and chopped
60g celery (1 stick), chopped
300ml Brown Chicken Stock (see page 280)
1 bay leaf
2 thyme sprigs
1 garlic clove, crushed
4 tsp rapeseed oil

For the stewed gooseberries
200g gooseberries, trimmed and halved
50g caster sugar

For the cabbage
200g Hispi cabbage, stem removed, sliced thick
3 tbsp water
10g unsalted butter
2 pinches white pepper

To serve
1 tsp arrowroot, diluted in 1 tbsp of cold water
12 gooseberries

Sit the pig cheeks in the white wine overnight.

Prepare the stewed gooseberries the next day. Put into a medium bowl with the sugar and macerate for 15 minutes then transfer to a medium saucepan on a medium heat and cook for 5 minutes, with a lid, at a gentle simmer, stirring to avoid catching on the bottom of the pan. Take off the heat, pour into a jug blender and blend on full speed for 1 minute until smooth. Taste and adjust with a splash of water if too acidic.

Preheat the oven to 120°C/Gas Mark ½. Drain the pig cheeks and reserve the liquor. Dry thoroughly.

To cook the pig cheeks, in a medium sauté pan on a medium heat, brown the meat in half the butter for 5 minutes, then add the onion, carrot, celery and remaining butter and continue to caramelise for 3 minutes. Transfer the meat and vegetables to a heavy-based casserole, add the reserved liquor, chicken stock, bay leaf, thyme and garlic and bring to a simmer. Cook in the oven for 3 hours. Once cooked, remove the cheeks from the liquor (reserve this), pat dry and cool for 20 minutes.

In a medium frying pan on a low heat, add the rapeseed oil then the pig cheeks, skin-side down, and fry for 15 minutes; turning every 5 minutes to ensure a crisp crackling.

Prepare the cabbage towards the end of the cheeks' cooking time. In a large saucepan on a high heat, bring all the ingredients to the boil, covered with a lid, and cook for 6 minutes.

To serve, in a large saucepan on a high heat, bring 300ml of the reserved cooking liquor to a boil and cook until reduced by a third. Stir in the arrowroot and bring to the boil for 1 minute, then remove from the heat and add the gooseberries. Steep the fruit in the sauce for 5 minutes. Carve the pig cheeks in half. Serve with a spoonful of stewed gooseberry purée, cabbage and steeped gooseberries. Spoon the cooking sauce over and around.

GREEN GOOSEBERRY JELLY CHEESECAKE WITH RED GOOSEBERRY COMPOTE

The Kew garden has enabled me to discover many British heritage fruit and vegetables, which had been unfamiliar to me. The tartness of a gooseberry is a strange concept for a Frenchman but the challenge of trying to conquer its sourness and create flavoursome dishes from it was attractive. I must modestly admit that I feel this cheesecake is a triumph and I'm now happy to adopt these northern green berries in my cooking. This dessert is based on two varieties of gooseberry – the gooseberry jelly, made using the green heritage variety Invicta, is dry and acidic; the accompanying compote is made from a hybrid red variety, Hinnomaki, which is much sweeter and I found it didn't need any sugar. This recipe has allowed me to celebrate the revival of an almost forgotten British culinary treasure; I feel a much better Frenchman for it.

SERVES 10–16

Preparation time: 40 minutes, plus chilling
Cooking time: 40 minutes

For the oat biscuit base
80g rye flour
100g wholemeal flour
80g unsalted butter
2g bicarbonate of soda
40g caster sugar
3g salt
95g jumbo oats
1 egg, beaten

For the filling
300g cream cheese
130g crème fraîche
1 tbsp Vanilla Purée (see page 281) or good-quality vanilla extract
juice of ¼ lemon, plus an extra drop for the egg whites
2 gelatine leaves

Preheat the oven to 180°C/Gas Mark 4. Have ready a 20 x 4cm pastry ring or cake tin.

For the oat biscuit base, put the flours, butter, bicarbonate of soda, sugar and salt in a large bowl. With your fingertips, crumble the ingredients together until the mixture resembles breadcrumbs. Add the oats and egg and mix well, then knead until it comes together.

With a rolling pin, roll the biscuit mixture out between two sheets of baking parchment to a thickness of 5mm. Lift on to a baking tray and remove the top piece of paper. Bake in the oven for 15 minutes.

Remove from the oven and leave to rest for 2 minutes. Using the pastry ring or cake tin, press down into the biscuit, cutting through the bottom. Leave to cool completely before using for the cheesecake. Remove the excess biscuit from around the ring; this can be used to crumble on top, if wished.

For the filling, in a large bowl mix the cream cheese, crème fraîche, vanilla purée or extract and lemon juice together.

Place the gelatine in a small saucepan with 2 teaspoons of water, melt over a gentle heat to a liquid. Once slightly cool, briskly whisk into the cream mixture.

Continued overleaf $\rightarrow$

Filling continued
100g caster sugar
5 tsp water
4 medium egg whites

For the gooseberry jelly
200g green gooseberries, washed,
    stalks removed and cut in half
10g caster sugar
2¼ gelatine leaves, softened in
    water then drained
50g water

For the topping
about 10–12 firm green
    gooseberries, stalks removed

In a small saucepan dissolve the sugar in the water, bring to a boil and continue to heat to 121°C.

Meanwhile, in a food mixer fitted with the whisk attachment or using an electric hand whisk and a bowl, whisk the egg whites, adding just a single drop of lemon juice at the beginning. Whisk to soft peaks.

Turn the whisk to a medium speed. The best technique for making this kind of Italian meringue is to pour the hot sugar syrup down the side of the bowl in a single thread so that it mixes beautifully. Otherwise the speed of the whisk will spin the sugar and solidify it over the whisk and bowl. Continue to whisk on a medium speed for a further 5 minutes until the mixture is glossy – the hot syrup will partially cook the egg white making it stable. Rest the base of the bowl in a bowl of iced water and continue to whisk by hand until the mixture is completely cool. When cool, add half the egg whites to the cream filling mixture and briskly beat with a whisk until smooth, then add the remaining egg whites and fold together.

Place the ring with the biscuit base on to a baking tray or plate and pour the filling into the ring, leaving a gap of 5mm from the top of the ring and level the surface flat using a palette knife or the back of a spoon. Refrigerate for 2 hours to allow the mixture to firm up before adding the gooseberry jelly.

For the gooseberry jelly, put the gooseberries into a bowl and macerate with the sugar for 15 minutes. Transfer to a small saucepan on a medium heat and simmer for 10 minutes, covered with a lid, then pour into a blender, with the softened gelatine and water and blend on full speed for 1 minute. To make sure the purée is smooth, pass it through a fine sieve into a bowl, forcing it through using the back of a ladle. Rest the base of the bowl over a bowl of iced water to cool, stirring all the time, and once the mixture starts to thicken, spoon it over the chilled cheesecake.

For the topping, top and tail the gooseberries and cut each one crossways into slices 2mm thick. Arrange 16 slices of

For the gooseberry compote
500g red gooseberries, trimmed
50g caster sugar (optional)

gooseberries around the edge of the cheesecake on top of the jelly. Chill the cheesecake overnight or until set completely.

For the compote, cut the gooseberries in half. Taste one – if sweet enough, there is no need to macerate them, if they are a little sour, put in a medium mixing bowl with the sugar and leave to macerate for 15 minutes.

Transfer to a medium saucepan on a medium heat and cook for 10 minutes with a lid on, stewing them at a gentle bubble; stir from time to time to prevent the compote catching on the bottom of the pan. Remove from the heat and allow to cool completely, taste and adjust with a splash of water if it's too acidic or a little sugar, if needed.

Serve the cheesecake with the compote alongside for your guests to help themselves.

Chef's note
Should you want to make the gooseberry flavour of the cheesecake stronger, you can stew 100g gooseberries until soft, then purée them and stir them into the filling mixture at the end.

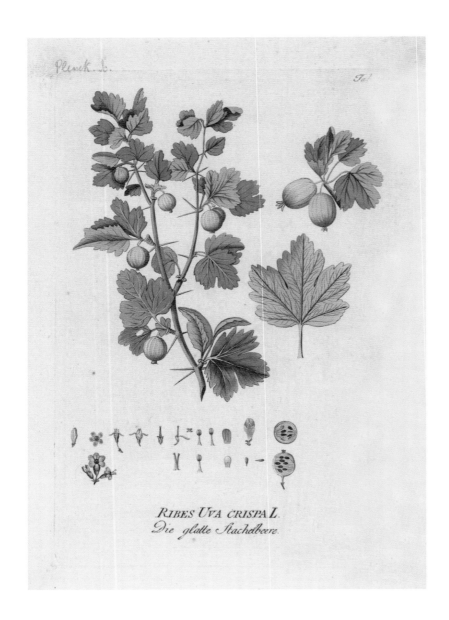

Gooseberry (Ribes uva-crispa) *from* Icones Plantarum Medicinalium, *vol.2: tab. 149 (1788-1812) by Joseph Jacob Plenck.*

STRAWBERRIES

'THE ENGLISH, LIKE THE FRENCH, have a huge love affair with strawberries,' says Raymond, 'but the irony is that when there are hundreds of different varieties, until relatively recently in England people have mostly been restricted to just one, the Elsanta. Loved by producers and supermarkets because it looks good and is a "keeper", it has a long shelf life and doesn't bruise easily. I resent that strawberry because it epitomises the relegation of food to an intensively-farmed commodity. It undermines all the principles of biodiversity and has persuaded people to accept the average, when they could have the sublime!

Wild, woodland strawberries have been enjoyed since antiquity, but the garden variety we know today only came into existence in the eighteenth century, thanks to a fluke cross-pollination of two wild native varieties from the Americas.

The good news, though, is that I truly believe there is a British strawberry flavour revival coming our way.' For Raymond, the strawberry on a pedestal, against which all others have to be measured, is the French Gariguette, with its 'most beautiful fresh, clean, intense, complex flavour and perfume, the perfect balance of sweetness and acidity. It is the first strawberry of the year, appearing in February, and in France we look forward to celebrating it in the same way as the first asparagus or the first garden pea. We tried some in the garden at Kew but they need sunshine and constant warmth in springtime whereas the summer weather in Britain can be unpredictable, so I doubt that they would have been a success. However, we will never know, because virtually all our strawberries suddenly and mysteriously disappeared. I arrived at the garden to taste them, and ended up like Inspector Clouseau, searching for evidence... Was it squirrels or visitors to the garden who couldn't resist the berries? The case will remain forever unsolved and the perpetrators never brought to justice! I hear that the Gariguette can grow quite well in Cornwall, but the risk with the British weather is that one good day here and there is not enough for them to develop their flavour, so they might look the same, but the taste: no, it can't compare to those grown in France.'

The 'garden' strawberry as we know it today only came into existence in the eighteenth century. However, wild, woodland strawberries have been enjoyed since antiquity, and the genus name *Fragaria* comes from the Latin word *fraga*, meaning fragrance. Like the raspberry, the strawberry actually belongs to the rose family (it is known as a 'false' fruit, as it has its seeds on the outside), and thanks to its red colour and heart shape it has long been linked with love and perfection. 'One of my most stunning memories is of the wild strawberries that grew near our family home in France,' says Raymond. 'At a certain moment of the year the woods were a vision of crimson: a carpet of strawberries, and above them the wild raspberries tumbling downwards, so laden were their bushes.'

In Medieval times, stone masons frequently carved strawberries into pillars and altars, while the idea of pairing strawberries and cream is

'Doubtless God could have made a better berry, but doubtless God never did', wrote Dr William Butler in the seventeenth century. He was referring to the small, woodland berries that were the only variety known until the following century.

thought to have begun during the lavish Tudor feasting enjoyed by the court of Henry VIII. By the seventeenth century, the English apothecary and writer, Dr William Butler, was famously declaring, 'Doubtless God could have made a better berry, but doubtless God never did.' Even though strawberries were being grown in gardens, the variety was still the small, fragrant woodland berry.

The first example of the 'garden' strawberry came about thanks to a chance cross-pollination of two native (wild) varieties from the Americas. *Fragaria virginiana*, an abundant and highly aromatic, but quite small strawberry native to North America, had been introduced to France in the seventeenth century and its popularity soon spread through Europe. Then in 1714, Amédée-François Frézier, a French scientist and engineer in the Army Intelligence Corps, travelled to Chile on a reconnaissance – some would say spying – mission, where he found a large, white, juicy, pineapple-flavoured variety of strawberry, 'as large as a whole walnut' and brought some plants home to France. When, by chance, decades later, some of the Chilean fruit, named *Fragaria chiloensis*, were planted amongst some *Fragaria virginiana* strawberries they cross-pollinated to produce a natural hybrid: an exciting new berry, large, like the Chilean variety, but with the more delicate flavour of *Fragaria virginiana*. In a nod to its pineappley character, the French botanist Antoine Nicolas Duchesne, who established a collection of strawberries in the gardens at Versailles, designated the new variety *Fragaria* x *ananassa* (*ananas* being the French for pineapple). From this first natural hybridisation of two native species, generations of cross-breeding and selection have followed to give us today's modern hybrids.

In nineteenth-century Britain, growers pioneered the breeding of strawberries on a large scale. The first truly commercial berry, Keens Seedling, was grown by market gardener Michael Keens and was so successful that it remained one of the most important British varieties for another century. In recent times, however, given the predominance of supermarket shopping, breeding has become more and more focused on high-yielding varieties that produce big fruit with a good shelf life, appear cosmetically perfect in the eyes of the consumer and are more tolerant to disease. Hence the rise and rise of the ubiquitous Elsanta. Frequently, however, the casualty in the process is the thrilling, rich, sweet-sharp burst of flavour that has captivated people all over the world for centuries.

Since 1983 the national programme for strawberry breeding has been based at the East Malling Research station in Kent. 'What they are doing there is so exciting,' says Raymond, 'because at last the emphasis is on flavour again. Thankfully, I believe retailers and growers are now responding to what the consumer really wants, which is berries that are grown not just for their beauty or their shelf life, but for their taste. I hope, soon, that that will also mean less sugar, because, like so much of our fruit, strawberries have been bred with too much emphasis on sweetness at the expense of the necessary balancing acidity.

'As we speak there are thousands of different strawberries being tested each year, with so many different flavour profiles: some lemony, some pineappley, some peachy, some even with raspberry notes. And the colours! There is everything from white to pale pink, to rich, dark woodland red. With my good friend William Sibley, the chairman of the East Malling Trust, I must have tasted 50 varieties. Of course some tasted flat, imbalanced or had no length of flavour; others were either too mushy or tight-textured, but some, like Buddy, were unbelievably brilliant.

'As much as I love to support heritage varieties, I understand that they are not always the best. So what they are achieving at East Malling is a perfect example of what science can do when it connects with taste; with the cook, the gardener and the wisdom and understanding that is passed from one generation to the next; with the soil and the climate – in order to give us wonderful strawberries again.'

Below: The search is continually on for a strawberry with the perfect balance of sweetness, acidity and fragrance.

GROWING NOTES

The advantage of growing your own strawberries, is that you are able to leave them on the plant until they are fully, juicily ripe, whereas a supermarket berry will always have to be picked earlier, chilled, transported to the store, and will then have to stay in good condition for several days. Growers of the Elsanta, say in its favour that if it is allowed to grow to rich, red, full ripeness and eaten straight after picking, it has a character and charm that elevates it way beyond its bland supermarket reputation.

It is important to buy plants from a certified source, to make sure they are disease free.

You can buy established plants in pots, however for planting out, strawberries are usually sold as 'bare-rooted runners': literally a root system with some leaves, which can be grown in beds, growbags or containers. Choose a sunny area with shelter from the wind.

For planting in beds, strawberries like a fertile, well-draining soil.

Prepare the beds three or four weeks in advance by digging in well-rotted manure or compost. Keep weed free.

Runners are intended to be planted at different times of year according to variety, so check when you buy. Also, if they have been kept in cold storage, you can usually plant them in late spring to midsummer and they should crop in around nine weeks. Other varieties (not cold-stored) can be planted in August so they can get established before winter and will be ready to pick the following summer.

Plant in lines (using a stretch of string as a guide, see picture opposite) leaving around 30–35cm between each runner.

With a trowel, dig a hole for each plant, big enough to comfortably accommodate the roots, and spread these out. You will see the 'crown' at the top of the roots. This should rest just on the surface of the soil. If you bury it beneath it might rot, and if it is too far above the surface the roots can spread above ground.

Water well when the plants are establishing themselves, during dry spells and when the fruit is ripening.

Surrounding the plants with straw helps to keep the soil warm, and if the plant is heavy with berries this will also protect them from drooping into the soil, so they stay clean and are less likely to rot.

If necessary, protect against frosts with horticultural fleece. If the plant is flowering during a frost, this can cause strawberry black eye. The central, reproductive parts of the flower will turn black, even though the petals stay white, and the fruit will not form properly.

'Net sturdily against birds and squirrels, preferably using a fruit cage,' says Alice. Be warned that squirrels love strawberries so much, they can be quite inventive in order to get at them! 'We want the garden to look as beautiful as possible, so we have used netting rather than cages,' she says, 'but we have a clever squirrel that has to be a suspect in the case of the disappearing strawberries! It hides during the daytime when visitors are in the

Good air circulation also helps protect against powdery mildew, which leaves a white coating on leaves, and fungal leaf spot, which causes brownish spots ringed with yellow on the foliage. As before, remove and dispose of any affected parts of the plant.

garden, then comes out when everyone has gone. I first spotted it when I was watering late one evening. Thinking it was caught in the net, I went to rescue it and realised that it had perfected a technique of sitting on top of the net above the strawberries, so that its weight lowered it down just enough to tuck into the berries through the net!'

Harvest fruit when they have a rich depth of colour (bear in mind the shade will vary with the variety) – and ideally on a warm day when their flavour will be at its best.

Botrytis is a common grey mould that affects strawberries and thrives on humidity. Good air circulation helps prevent it, which is why it is best not to crowd plants together. Remove any affected leaves, buds and flowers and dispose of them.

After harvest, cut older leaves back to 5–7.5cm to reduce the risk of disease for the following year, leaving any new growth, and also cut away any thin runners that the plant has put out above the ground.

The plants will tend to be less productive after three years, so it is a good idea to replace them with new ones at this stage and plant them in a different area of the garden to help prevent disease from building up.

Left: Although there is no connection between straw and the name strawberry, a surrounding of straw helps to keep the soil warm in the strawberry beds. If the plants become heavy with berries the straw will also protect them from drooping into the soil, so they will stay clean and are less likely to rot.

RAYMOND'S FLAVOUR NOTES

For me, the best strawberry will always be the Gariguette for its perfume and complexity. It is also the earliest.

I also love the wild, woodland strawberry – the woods around our village were covered in them when I was growing up. And they grow so well in gardens. They are like tiny, tiny perfumed jewels. You have to be very patient to pick them, but if you leave a bowl of them in a room, their scent takes over.

The other strawberry I love is the Mara des Bois, which was developed by grower Jacques Marionnet on the farm now run by his son Pascal in France, where they also grow the Gariguette. The Mara des Bois was bred in the 1990s, and the idea was to produce fruit that is the size of the modern garden strawberry, but with all the beautiful perfume and flavour of the wild woodland berry.

Of the older British varieties, one of the best I have tasted is Royal Sovereign: what a strawberry. And of the newer ones, Buddy, Marshmello and Albion from East Malling Research.

Please, please, don't eat strawberries straight from the fridge as the cold dulls the flavour. Take them out and leave them for at least an hour and they will taste so much better.

When a strawberry is beautiful, in one way you don't want to do anything with it except eat it all by itself, or with some wonderful Jersey double cream, but equally, you could preserve all its flavour in the simplest sorbet. Just purée the fruit, add a tiny touch of sugar and leave it to macerate it for 20 minutes, then squeeze in some lemon juice, a little pepper and churn in an ice-cream machine.

Right: Strawberry plants in flower and bearing fruit in the garden at Kew; and opposite, as depicted in Joseph Jacob Plenck's Icones Plantarum, *vol. 5.*

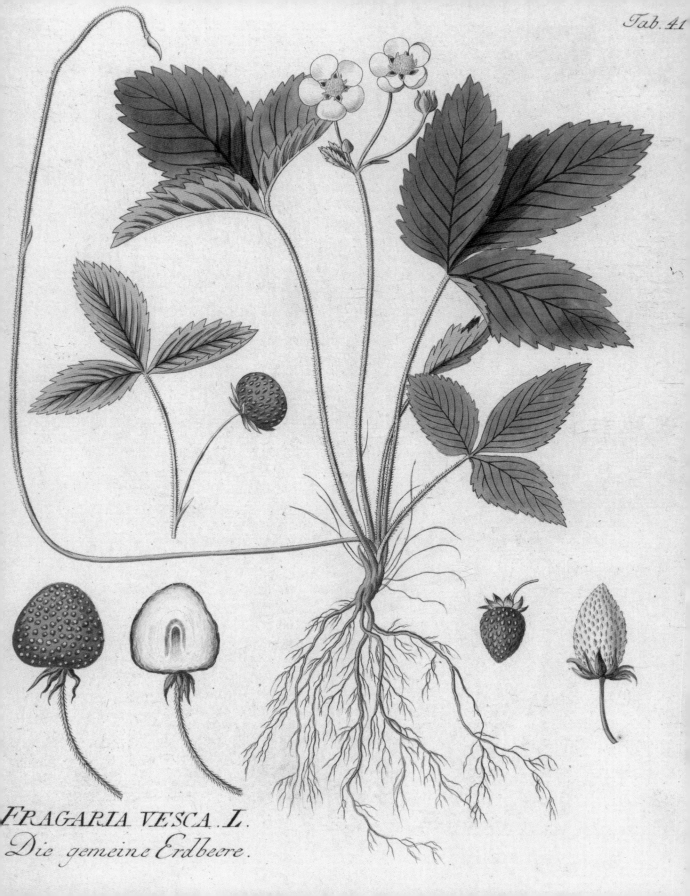

Tab. 41.

FRAGARIA VESCA. L.
Die gemeine Erdbeere.

LOW-SUGAR STRAWBERRY JAM

I have wonderful memories of the strawberry season when my mum would make jam and the whole house would be taken over by the aroma. Feeding five children meant that her jam-making was a small cottage industry and she would make about 10 litres at a time. She would skim off the froth from the top – that's the part we children would get to eat first; it was simply delicious.

It has always disturbed me to see so much sugar in jams. Though my pâtissiers didn't approve, many years ago I waged war on sugar and the quantities we were using in my kitchen, and I won! So now my pâtissiers are happy to make a low-sugar jam. And the result is that the jam is more colourful and certainly less sweet so the fruit flavour triumphs.

MAKES 900G

Preparation time: 10 minutes
Cooking time: 25 minutes

For the jam
900g strawberries (Buddy,
    Gariguette or
    Mara des Bois), chopped
250g caster sugar
7g pectin (see Chef's note)
4 tbsp water
3 tsp lemon juice

To seal the jars
80ml kirsch liqueur

To prepare the jam, in a small bowl, macerate the strawberries in 230g of the sugar for 15 minutes. The sugar will permeate the fruit, provide better texture and increase the flavour.

In a large, heavy-based saucepan on a medium heat, bring the macerated strawberries to a gentle simmer. Skim off any froth that rises to the surface and cook until broken down.

In a small bowl, mix together the remaining 20g of sugar, the pectin and water and leave to one side for 15 minutes for the sugar to absorb the water and form a paste. Stir the paste into the warm strawberries and bring to the boil for 3 minutes.

To test if the jam is the right consistency, pour a tablespoon on to a plate and put into the fridge for 10 minutes. Turn off the heat under the jam. The jam is set if it wrinkles when you push your finger into it. If the jam isn't quite setting, bring it back to the boil for 5 minutes and repeat the test. Once the jam is at a setting consistency, stir in the lemon juice and set to one side to cool slightly before pouring into sterilised jars (see page 18).

To create an airtight seal, gently warm a small pan with the kirsch and using a long match or lighter set it alight, then pour a layer over the jam. Quickly screw on each lid and leave to cool. This will create a bacteria-free vacuum inside the jar. Unopened, you can store the jam in a cool dark place for up to two months. Once open, keep refrigerated and use within two weeks.

Chef's note
I have found that apple pectin is the best because it has the strongest binding than any other I've tried.

FROZEN STRAWBERRY TARTLETS WITH VANILLA WHIPPED CREAM AND MERINGUE

A new dish is always an exciting and rewarding moment for any cook, but there is a lot of trial and error to get it just as you've imagined it; even down to writing the recipe. After countless re-working, I think this recipe is the perfect iced tart and in making it you will undoubtedly be greatly admired by your guests. It's a little bit demanding but worth the challenge – both in terms of appearance and flavour. You will notice that I've replaced sugar with stevia. Actually at one stage I believed I'd discovered stevia. Seven years ago I tasted a very sweet plant and thought that it was completely unique; it tasted at least 20 times sweeter than sugar. Then when I started to read about stevia, I discovered it had no calories and didn't raise your blood sugar level. I spent days trying to make the herb into syrups and to crystallise it. Except that... I went to my local retailer and there it was on the shelf, transformed into a sweetener that is actually 250 times sweeter than sugar!

Many people claim that stevia has got a particular flavour that interferes with cooking; I generally disagree. It takes a very special palate to tell the difference and I've tried it on many people. If you use stevia, ensure that you don't mistake it for 'truvia' which is stevia mixed with quite a large amount of sugar. Of course, stevia doesn't have the same properties as sugar so what stevia can't do is recreate the beauty of a whipped meringue!

SERVES 4

Preparation time: 1 hour 30 minutes

You will also need: 4 x 7.5cm pastry rings and 4 x 6cm pastry rings; 25 x 5cm acetate to line the insides of the frame; and a squeezy plastic bottle

For the sorbet
450g strawberries (my favourites are Buddy, Gariguette, Royal Sovereign or Mara des Bois), stalks removed
1 tsp stevia powder
dash of lemon juice

Take four 7.5cm pastry rings and tightly stretch cling film over the top of each one, then turn them upside down; these will become the frames for the tarts. Line a tray with greaseproof paper, place the pastry rings on the tray with the cling film on the bottom, line the insides with the acetate plastic and transfer to the freezer.

For the sorbet, in a large bowl macerate the strawberries with the stevia and lemon juice for 30 minutes. Macerating the strawberries will give the sorbet much more flavour.

Blend the strawberries to a purée. Set aside 150g of the purée for the coulis. Pour the remaining strawberry purée into a squeezy plastic bottle, then squeeze the purée into the bottom of each frozen ring until 5mm deep. Return the tray to the freezer and leave for 30 minutes until frozen solid.

Remove from the freezer and place a 6cm pastry ring on top of each frozen purée, in the centre, and press it down gently so that it just indents the base. Squeeze more purée into the gap between the two rings, to create a wall 2cm high.

Continued overleaf →

For the tart filling

200g strawberries (Buddy, Gariguette, Royal Sovereign or Mara des Bois), cut into small dice
large pinch of stevia powder

For the crème Chantilly

100g whipping cream
large pinch of stevia powder
½ tsp Vanilla Purée (see page 281) or good-quality vanilla extract

To serve

50g miniature meringues, crush 4–6 of them
100g Low-sugar Strawberry Jam (see page 152)
4 mint sprigs
6 strawberries, halved

Place back in the freezer and leave to freeze for at least 2 hours, until solid. (The steps up to this stage can be done a few days in advance.) Place 4 serving plates in the freezer 1 hour prior to serving.

For the filling, in a medium bowl macerate the strawberries with the stevia for 30 minutes.

Meanwhile, make the crème Chantilly by whipping the cream with the stevia and vanilla purée or extract, until firm peaks form. Beware, if you over-whip the cream, it will separate and you will create butter!

Mix 100g of the reserved coulis with the strawberries. Fold half the macerated strawberries through the Chantilly cream. Reserve the other half for decorating the top of the cake.

Take one sorbet out of the freezer. Remove the inner pastry ring by rubbing your fingers around the inside to soften the sorbet behind it slightly and enable you to gently lift off the ring. Now lift off the outer pastry ring and gently peel away the acetate surrounding the sorbet. Return each sorbet case to a baking tray in the freezer as you repeat this process for the remaining sorbets.

When ready to serve, remove the plates from the freezer and place a small amount of the crushed meringue in the centre of each plate to stop the tarts from sliding around, then cover with a frozen sorbet case. Place a spoonful of the jam in the bottom of each sorbet case, followed by the strawberry and Chantilly cream mix. Finish each tart by topping a spoonful of the reserved macerated strawberries, followed by a few whole meringues and mint leaves. Drizzle the remaining reserved coulis around each tart, place a few halved strawberries on the plates and serve immediately.

TOMATOES

DRAMATICALLY DIFFERENT IN APPEARANCE, it is sometimes hard to believe that

the tomato and the potato belong to the same botanical family and have a similar history. Both originate from South America and in the case of tomatoes, the predecessors of the Aztecs and Incas were cultivating them as early as AD700. Both have become hugely popular the world over – tomato seeds have even been grown in space – and both were originally viewed in some quarters with suspicion.

The tomato plant, like its relative the potato, suffered the sting of suspicion when first seen in Britain in the sixteenth century.

First introduced to Europe by the Spanish in the 1500s, the earliest tomato plants to be grown were most likely ornamental. In France the brightly coloured orbs inspired the romantic name of *pomme d'amour* – apple of love; in Italy *pomodoro* – golden apple, the name that remains today and which suggested that the first varieties were golden-yellow, rather than red.

The British, however, were not so easily wooed. The reason? Both the potato and tomato are members of the nightshade family and the botanists of the time classified the tomato plant alongside another nightshade, the poisonous mandrake. Ancient fruits of both, preserved in jars in the Kew herbarium show that there was in fact a striking resemblance.

While John Gerard, in his first edition of *The Herball* of 1597, acknowledged that the Spanish and Italians had advanced from admiring to eating the fruit 'boiled with pepper, salt and oile', he described the tomato plant as 'of ranke and stinking savour... Colde, yea perhaps in the highest degree of coldeness', most likely referring to 'cold' in relation to the four 'humours' that it was believed had to be kept in balance for the health of the body. Even a century later the French botanist Joseph Pitton de Tournefort noted in *The Compleat Herbal*, published after his death, that 'considering their great Moisture and Coldness, the Nourishment they afford must be bad'. However the juice could be used to cure 'Rheum or defluxion of hot humours upon the eyes'.

Botanists and horticulturists continued to have their doubts as to the place of the tomato, other than as an attractive curiosity, for another century. However, tomato recipes, especially sauces, gradually began to find their way into French cooking, and by Victorian times had been absorbed into the British repertoire, partly due to the influence of French cuisine on the moneyed classes, and also of Jewish communities with Spanish heritage, trading connections and a history of cooking with tomatoes. By the time Mrs Beeton wrote her *Book of Household Management*, she was able to pronounce that the tomato was 'of immense importance in the culinary art', and 'almost universally approved' in sauces, soup and 'ketchup'.

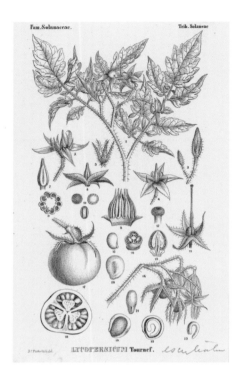

Above: Illustration of tomatoes (Solanum lycopersicum) *from the 1845 edition of* Genera Plantarum Florae Germanicae, *(vol 4: p.349) by the German botanist and pharmacologist, Theodor Friedrich Ludwig Nees von Esenbeck (1787–1837).*

'I grew up with two varieties of tomato,' says Raymond. 'Coeur de Boeuf, which was a hefty, heart-shaped, pointed tomato – really magnificent – and smooth as well; and the Marmande, which was much more misshapen, often with cracks inside; still quite big, but half the size of the Coeur de Boeuf.

'My job was to prepare the ground for them, water them, tie them up, look after their every need, so I felt I had an incredible relationship with them. Even after all these years, I look at the life of a sun-ripened tomato and I think it is such a luxury to have this delicacy. Imagine all the love from the gardener to help it through its risky life, avoiding blight and the predators that are everywhere, to grow into a beautiful ripe fruit.

'Both the Coeur de Boeuf and Marmande were brilliant for salads and for stuffing. My mother would take out the centre and keep it to one side for the sauce. Then she would stuff the cavity with minced lamb, beef or sometimes fish, mixed with chopped vegetables, breadcrumbs, plenty of garlic, parsley, thyme and a bay leaf. Finally, she would chop up the tomato flesh that she had removed, mix it with a little olive oil and tomato purée and spoon it into the base of an ovenproof dish. The stuffed tomatoes were placed on top and then the dish went into the oven. When it came to the table, you would eat the tomatoes and mop up the thick sauce with bread.

'I can get very emotional about tomatoes, but the sad reality is that at least 90 per cent of those sold today are bred for their uniform looks and shelf life and are grown in huge greenhouses, hydroponically (without soil), with nutrients and often chemicals fed into the base of the vine. When tomatoes on the vine first appeared in supermarkets I couldn't understand how they could all be uniformly ripe, when my own tomatoes were all at different stages: some would be green and unripe, some just turning red, others over-ripe. How did they do that? Of course what happens is that commercial growers take the vines from the plant before they are ripe. The vines can then be cooled, stored and transported to distribution plants, where they are ripened in special chambers using ethylene gas. There is nothing scary about that, since ethylene is a plant hormone produced naturally in most fruit, but it is a totally artificial process, and the flavour cannot be as intense as in a tomato ripened in the garden or in soil in the greenhouse.'

In order to illustrate the difference in flavour, Raymond and the team at Kew grew a selection of heritage tomatoes, in different shapes, sizes and colours, then tested them against shop-bought tomatoes, with the help of Kew scientist Monique Simmonds. In answer to Raymond's complaint that modern varieties of fruit are often bred to be too sweet, Monique explains that in the case of tomatoes, the process of breeding uniform-looking fruits has resulted in the reduction of the diversity of compounds that provide the tomatoes with flavour, which results in a sweet, rather bland, tomato. Furthermore, she points out that when tomatoes are grown organically, they are forced to defend themselves against pests more fervently than mass-produced tomatoes, which can be sprayed with herbicides and pesticides. As a result, they may produce more compounds which contribute to their taste and health properties. For the experiment, garden-grown varieties and comparable shop-bought ones were pulped and filtered to extract the important compounds for Monique to analyse.

Above: Marmande tomatoes are old favourites with Raymond for salads and stuffing.

The results showed that some of the home-grown tomatoes contained far more sugar than their supermarket equivalents. Interestingly, the sweetest of all proved to be Gardener's Delight cherry tomatoes, which contained almost three times as much natural sugar as their mass-produced counterparts. 'We have grown a virtual sugar lump of a tomato!' says Joe. Furthermore, over and above the flavour element, the graph of Monique's analysis showed that each of the Kew-grown tomatoes that were tested registered more peaks than the supermarket ones – each peak representing potentially health-improving compounds. 'What more enticement do you need to plant some seeds and grow your own beautiful tomatoes?' asks Raymond.

Left: Twenty-three varieties of tomato were grown outdoors at Kew, in a bed that also included five colourful varieties of Swiss chard: Rainbow chard, Rhubarb chard, Fordhook Giant White Silver and Flamingo; as well as calendula (yellow and orange forms) and basil (Thai and Sweet Genovese).

GROWING NOTES

You can either grow bush tomatoes or taller 'cordon' plants that grow upwards from a single stem and can be supported by a cane. Or in greenhouses, they can be entwined around ropes stretched from the floor to the rafters.

If you are going to grow your tomatoes outside in beds, dig in some well-rotted manure or compost a few weeks beforehand.

When planting from seed, it is best to start them off in module trays as these allow the roots to develop well before transplanting and you can pop them out easily with the minimum of root disturbance. Fill the modules with compost, then plant two seeds in each one. Cover with a fine layer of compost and water in.

Within a few weeks the seedlings will have emerged, and once they have two leaves, if both seeds have germinated, thin to just one seedling, snipping off the other at the base (don't be tempted to leave both, as they will compete with each other for nutrients and light). Once the thinned seedlings have reached four leaves, they are ready to be transferred to bigger individual pots. Tomato plants benefit from this 'potting on' before planting out in beds, as the more confined space of the pot promotes growth. Make a hole in the centre of a pot of compost using a dibber (the pointed tool for making holes for seeds and bulbs) then push each module out from the base and lower into the hole. Firm in and water lightly.

When the seedlings have grown into a leafy plant of around 30cm tall, you can transfer them to your prepared beds (or large containers if you are growing them outside in a small space or under glass). If you really want to maximise the growth – and yield – take off the lower leaves and dig as deep a hole as you can so you can plant the stem up to the higher growth. Water in well.

Once you see the flower trusses forming, restrict each plant to five or six of these trusses and regularly pinch off any side shoots and the leaves below the lowest truss. Also stop the plant from growing any higher by pinching out the growing tip. By doing all this, you focus the plant's energy on producing less, but better, fruit. It is best to do the trimming in the mornings when the stems are turgid with sap and will snap off cleanly.

Trimming the plant in this way also means that it won't get bushy, so the air circulation will be better, as blight can be more of a problem in congested conditions. Like potatoes, which are a member of the same family (Solanaceae), tomatoes are genetically susceptible to the particular pathogen that causes blight, so if there are any spores left in the garden from a previous crop of either tomatoes or potatoes this can increase the risk. For this reason it is a good idea not to grow any crops in the family in the same place year after year. (If you are growing tomatoes in a greenhouse and you have a problem with blight, wash out the greenhouse with soapy water in the winter before growing any more tomatoes the following season).

A common enemy of tomatoes grown under glass is the white fly. 'And the only thing it likes better than tomatoes is basil,' says Joe. 'So by "companion" planting basil nearby, you hope to entice the white fly to go for that instead. To be effective, plant three basil plants per tomato plant – hopefully you will get some basil too!'

Right: Ripening Orange Banana tomatoes, and far right, the Darby Striped Yellow/Green variety will ripen to a yellowy-orange with green stripes, and is wonderful in salads (see page 166).

RAYMOND'S FLAVOUR NOTES

Different tomato varieties are suited to different uses in the kitchen.

For sauces, Italians will look for San Marzano or Roma, never a Marmande. Why? Because the Marmande has lots of juice, pips (which represent the high level of acidity), and water, so it would take far too long for the moisture to evaporate and for the tomatoes to reduce into a thick paste so the flavour would lose its freshness. If you slice a San Marzano in half, it has hardly any pips and hardly any water; it is mostly flesh, so it can be turned into a paste in no time and with its high level of sugar it is perfect for a tomato sauce.

For stuffing you need a tomato with a quite thick wall of skin, which is why the Marmande and Coeur de Boeuf work best. You could never stuff a Black Russian, for example, as it has a thin skin, but it is brilliant in a salad: compact, powerful in flavour and with a rich perfume.

For salad, my favourite varieties are Marmande, Coeur de Boeuf, Black Russian and Darby Striped Yellow/Green.

At one time, I thought of cherry tomatoes only as designer fruit, but I changed my mind when I created 'tomato essence', which has become famous all over the world. The story of how it came about is very lovely. It goes back to the salad my mum used to make. She would slice the tomatoes, dress them with oil and a little vinegar and salt and pepper and leave them for a little while, so that the salt would cure the tomatoes and extract some of the juices. The juices would form a pool in the bottom of the dish and all of us children would fight to dip our bread into them. The taste was divine and I always wanted to create something that would celebrate that purity of tomato flavour. But how?

One day I saw one of my chefs making a fruit jelly, using a jelly bag, hung so that the compression from the fruits forced the clear juice through. That was it: I had my idea. And when I got the recipe right and the essence began to drip through – *mon Dieu,* **what a flavour! The pure heart of the tomato.** It took me months to decide on the right variety. I decided it had to be cherry tomatoes, because they have a high ratio of juice to flesh and more sweetness than other tomatoes. In our taste tests of the cherry tomatoes grown at Kew, the two that came out top were Golden Currant and everybody's favourite, Gardener's Delight.

HERITAGE TOMATO AND MOZZARELLA SALAD

This salad is one of the simplest and is probably almost as old as the world, yet its success relies on using the ripest tomatoes. I have chosen four of the tastiest varieties – the Marmande, Coeur de Boeuf, the delicious Darby Striped Yellow/Green and the amazing Black Russian. They are perfect for salad, each of them sun-ripened, juicy and fleshy.

SERVES 6–8 AS A STARTER

Preparation time: 15 minutes

For the tomatoes
1.2kg heritage tomatoes
    (Marmande, Coeur de Boeuf,
    Darby Striped Yellow/Green
    and Black Russian)
1 Rose de Roscoff onion, cut into
    3mm slices
20 basil leaves, roughly chopped
3 tbsp finely chopped chives
1 garlic clove, chopped
2 tbsp white wine vinegar
6 tbsp extra virgin olive oil
sea salt and freshly ground black
    pepper

For the salad
1 head Freckles lettuce, leaves
    picked
1 head Seurat lettuce, leaves picked
1 head Lollo Rosso lettuce, leaves
    picked
1 head Reine des Glaces lettuce,
    leaves picked
1 tbsp white wine vinegar
2 tbsp extra virgin olive oil, plus a
    little extra to finish
3 x 120g buffalo mozzarella
50g Kalamata olives, pitted, dried
    in the oven for 1 hour at
    100°C/Gas Mark ¼,
    finely chopped

For the tomatoes, using a small paring knife, cut the hard core out of each tomato, then cut each into quarters. Transfer to a large bowl. Season with a pinch each of salt and pepper. Stir so the seasoning lightly cures the tomatoes, which will then produce a beautiful juice. Mix in the onion, herbs, garlic, vinegar and oil. Stir and leave to marinate for a minimum of 10 minutes for the flavours to infuse.

For the salad, at the last moment, mix the leaves in a large bowl. Season with a pinch each of salt and pepper, then toss the leaves with the vinegar and olive oil.

Arrange the leaves on a large platter. With a large spoon, lift the tomato mixture on to the salad. Cut the mozzarella in half and scatter around the salad. Sprinkle over the dried olives and finish with a drizzle of your best extra virgin olive oil. Gastronomy can be as simple as that... when you have wonderful produce.

GREEN TOMATO CHUTNEY

There is always a time when the summer is gone, most of the tomatoes have ripened beautifully, but a few have decided to stay green. As my mother would say, 'thou shalt not waste'. There are so many wonderful ways you can use these tomatoes: in jams, pickles or in a beautiful chutney. This wonderful condiment was completely alien to me until I came to Britain and enjoyed a piece of York ham served with a sweet fruity chutney. And now I've come to have huge admiration for this preserve, which can take on hundreds of different guises depending on the fruits, vegetables and spices used. I serve chutney with everything I can.

One of my biggest failures in life is not having found a way to replicate the smell of a raw tomato, cut from the vine: one of the greatest scents in the world. I would love it to burst out from a chutney like this. I have spent many weeks trying to capture or reinvent that smell – through steaming, simmering and making consommés. So if any of you have solved this mystery, please, do let me know.

MAKES 2 SMALL JAM JARS
(ABOUT 550G IN TOTAL)

Preparation time: 5 minutes
Cooking time: 20 minutes

For the chutney
500g green tomatoes, roughly
   chopped
100ml white wine vinegar
75g caster sugar
1 tsp yellow mustard seeds
2g pink peppercorns
1 red chilli, deseeded and thinly
   sliced
100g white onion, roughly diced
100ml water
½ tsp ground coriander seeds
pinch sea salt

In a medium saucepan on a medium heat, place all the ingredients and cook for 10 minutes covered with a lid.

Remove the lid, turn the heat to high and continue to cook for a further 7–8 minutes, stirring occasionally, until the chutney has reduced to a compote consistency. Remove from the heat and allow to cool at room temperature.

Once cool, taste and adjust the seasoning if required, then store in the fridge where it will keep for up to three weeks.

Serve with a mature Cheddar, such as a Montgomery, or a creamy blue cheese, such as a Stichelton. As a Frenchman I would also suggest that a great Comté, Roquefort, Bleu de Gex or any of the other 400 French cheeses will go very well with this chutney.

Chef's note
This chutney is very light in vinegar and low in sugar. Vinegar is the preservative that enables you to keep chutneys for many months, but this recipe doesn't contain enough to allow you to store the chutney for more than three weeks. On the other hand, it will be beautifully rounded and fresh without the sharp acidity that comes from recipes that contain a lot of vinegar.

When you make something spicy, acidic or sweet, the flavouring will feel much stronger while the dish is hot so be aware of this when you test your chutney. It may taste a little fierce at first but the spicing will mellow.

An illustration of 'false tomato', Solanum pseudolycopersicum *- a member of the vast* Solanacae *family. From* Hortus botanicus Vindobonensis, *vol. 1: t. 11 (1770) by Nikolaus Joseph von Jacquin, Dutch professor of botany and chemistry, and director of the botanical gardens at the University of Vienna.*

ONIONS

THE unsung heroes of the kitchen, onions are frequently taken for granted, pushed into the shade by more colourful and adventurous ingredients, but without them, where would we find the depth, sweetness and body that is at the heart of so many dishes around the world? Like a true team player, the onion brings out the best in its fellow vegetables, yet rarely gets the credit. It wasn't always so. The ancient Egyptians saw the onion's spherical shape as a symbol of eternity and it was considered so important that, along with garlic, whole onions were used in the mummification process and enclosed in tombs.

Onions are the modest ingredient of the kitchen, less glamorous than others, but essential in cooking all around the world.

The exact origins of the onion are blurred; some say it hails from central Asia, others from Iran or Pakistan, however historians agree that it has been cultivated for around 4,000 years or more, and there are references to the use of onion in medicine and food in ancient Chinese and Indian manuscripts, and in the Roman recipe collection, *Apicius De Re Coquinaria* (see page 68). Indeed, it was most likely the Romans who introduced the onion to Europe.

'My favourite is the Rose de Roscoff,' says Raymond. 'So beautiful to cook with, it is the perfect variety for onion soup, because it has real character.' Grown in Brittany since the seventeenth century, such is the individual nature of the pink Roscoff onion that in 2009 it was awarded the mark of 'appellation d'origine contrôllée' (AOC) recognising its distinctive character and regionality. It is also the variety that was popularised by the famous 'Onion Johnnies' who began bringing strings of them over to England in the nineteenth century. The nickname is said to come from the fact that many of the sellers had the first name Jann, the Breton version of Jean. Invariably wearing berets and sometimes striped tops, they pedalled around the country selling the onions from door to door, sparking the caricature image of the Frenchman that has prevailed ever since.

The first intrepid onion seller to make the trip by boat was Henri Olivier, in 1828, and it was so successful that he inspired more to follow in his footsteps. In November 1905 tragedy struck when the steamship the SS *Hilda* sank off St Malo and around 70 Johnnies who were among the passengers lost their lives. However, more and more continued to make the cross-channel trip, until, in the heyday of selling in the 1920s and 30s there were some 1,500 or so Johnnies – and at least one female 'Jenny' – travelling from Brittany to England, Wales and Scotland each year.

'Even as late as the 1970s, when I first came to England,' says Raymond, 'I saw them in Oxford, with their beautiful strings of onions loaded around their handlebars, and often the guys were quite drunk. I don't know how they stayed on their bikes!'

Left: Strings of Rose de Roscoff onions from Britanny were famously pedalled around Britain and sold on doorsteps by 'Onion Johnnies' on pushbikes (see page 172).

Above: Pink Rose de Roscoff onions have a colourful history, see page 172, and left, a few dry, sunny days allow the harvested onions to dry out on top of the beds before using, or drying further ready for storing.

GROWING NOTES

Onions like a sunny, sheltered site and well-drained soil.

Dig in compost or well-rotted manure the autumn before planting as, like garlic, onions don't enjoy freshly-manured ground.

Onions can be grown either from seed or 'sets', which are baby onions whose development has been arrested. Sets store up energy in the bulbs so they grow quicker, but they can be prone to bolting – focussing their energy into producing a stalk and flowerhead instead of forming a bulb. To avoid this, you can buy sets that have been heat-treated to kill off the flower embryo.

If growing from seed, sow between late February and early April in shallow rows – only around 1.5cm deep – and leave 30cm between the rows. (You can also start the seeds off indoors in modules: three seeds to each, thinning to one as the seedlings grow. Plant the seedlings out once their roots fill the module.)

If growing from sets, pull off any loose skin around the tips that would enable swooping birds to grab hold of them, and push the sets into the ground, up to their necks, so that their tips are just showing – again, no more, or the birds will pull them up – and firm the earth around them. Leave a space of 10cm between each one, and again, if planting in rows, leave 30cm between each row.

Cover sets with horticultural fleece until the leaves begin to form, to help fend off the birds.

If you have planted seeds, once the seedlings come through, thin out the rows so that you are left with plants that are 5cm apart, and then when they have reached pencil thickness, thin again until you have 10cm between each growing onion. This is important as overcrowded beds can heighten humidity and increase the plants' susceptibility to onion downy mildew (see below).

Like garlic and leeks, onions are susceptible to onion white rot and leek rust (see page 117 for more about these potential problems).

In addition, particularly during wet weather, the crop can be affected by onion downy mildew, which causes the leaves to turn yellow and for grey-ish patches of mould to form, which then turn purplish-brown. There is no control and if the mildew gets inside the onion bulb it will tend to shrivel and sprout quickly when stored. 'You can help to avoid the onset by keeping beds weed free and not growing the onions too close together, so that you can keep a good airflow around them,' advises Joe.

Harvest in late June and July. You will see the leaves begin to turn yellow and start to bend over. At this point wait for around 2–3 weeks, before lifting carefully with a garden fork. Do this during a dry, sunny spell, when you can leave the onions on top of the beds for 1–2 days to dry (see picture opposite).

You can use them straight away but of course the great thing about onions is that you can store them. Choose blemish-free bulbs and leave them somewhere airy until the leaves dry out completely and the skins become papery. Then, if you like, you can tie them all together to make an onion string to hang in the kitchen.

RAYMOND'S FLAVOUR NOTES

When the onion is the hero of the dish, my favourite is the Rose de Roscoff, which you can trust to deliver real character, for example in an onion soup or for stuffing.

For general cooking I use a white onion, as it is sweeter and caramelises better than a red onion, which I find sharper and more aggressive. A favourite is Ailsa Craig, a Scottish heritage onion from 1887, and one of the best white onions I ever tasted was in Alsace where I made an onion tart with the local Mulhouse onion.

For salads, I like to use a milder red onion, such as the Brunswick heritage variety (1870), cut very finely.

You have to respect an onion. It is a powerful weapon of flavour, but it has to be tamed through cooking, because it is full of substances that can make you cry and give you flatulence.

The reason that onions can make you cry when you chop or slice them is that as you pierce the cells, you activate the enzyme allinase, which sets off a chemical reaction to produce sulphurous compounds. These are released as a fine spray of microscopic 'bombs', which irritate the eyes and signal to our tear glands to wash the irritants away. Believe me, I have seen so many grown men crying like babies when chopping onions.

An onion's ability to induce tears may depend on its age – an older, more pungent one will often be the worst.

There are all sorts of tricks that people swear by to stop an onion from making you cry, but really the best thing is to use a very sharp knife, and chop as swiftly and cleanly as possible, so that you cause the least damage to the cells as you cut into them.

The British have an exquisite word, 'sweetening', which is not in the French vocabulary. Sweetening is exactly what you do when you take a rough, vulgar, sulphurous onion and apply heat to it through the medium of butter or oil to draw out its sugars.

Sometimes, if you are using onions as the base of a dish, rather than as the hero, you only want to cook them very gently for 10–15 minutes, until they become translucent and soften and sweeten, but don't brown.

At other times, for example in the onion soup opposite, you want to brown and caramelise the onions to achieve a richer, deeper intense flavour. To do this you first have to reduce all the moisture – and therefore the volume – from them. This will take about 20 minutes of gentle cooking in butter, and at first the onions will seem to release too much water into your pan. Don't panic, as this will gradually evaporate. Then you can turn up the heat a little until the onions brown and take on sweet aromas and flavours.

FRENCH ONION SOUP

Simple as it is, I think this is one of the greatest soups in the world. I make some croutons, then take some grated two-year-old Comté cheese; I float the croutons in the soup and cover the top of them with the cheese – generously! Heaven. I get quite emotional thinking about it.

SERVES 4

Preparation time: 25 minutes
Cooking time: 1 hour 10 minutes

For the soup
2 tbsp plain flour
60g unsalted butter
1kg Rose de Roscoff onions or white onions, cut into 3mm slices
2 tsp sea salt
2 pinches freshly ground black pepper
200ml dry white wine, boiled for 30 seconds (see Chef's note overleaf)
1.5 litres cold water
1 tsp caster sugar (optional)

For the croutons
12 x 1cm-slices baguette
150g Comté cheese (ideally two-year-old), grated

Preheat the oven to 170°C/Gas Mark 3½.

For the soup, put the flour into a small baking tin and toast in the oven for 30 minutes. Toasting the flour cooks the starch and develops a nutty flavour, which will add another layer of flavour to your soup.

On a high heat, in a large, non-stick saucepan, melt the butter without letting it brown. Add the onions and soften for 5 minutes, stirring frequently. Season with the salt and pepper.

Continue cooking the onions for 20–30 minutes to achieve an even, rich brown colour. Stir every 2–3 minutes and make sure you scrape any caramelised bits of onion from the base of the pan to prevent burning and achieve an even colour.

Once the onions are the desired colour, stir in the toasted flour and mix thoroughly to absorb all the juices. Gradually stir in the white wine, and one third of the cold water and whisk to prevent lumps forming. Bring to the boil, add the remaining water and simmer for 5 minutes. Taste and correct the seasoning, adding the sugar if required.

To make the croutons, heat your grill on a high setting. Arrange the baguette slices on a baking tray and toast on one side for 3–4 minutes, until lightly golden.

To serve, divide the soup between serving bowls, top with croutons, toasted side up, and sprinkle over the grated Comté.

Continued overleaf $\rightarrow$

Chef's notes

The quality of the onions you choose for this recipe is crucial.
You want both high acidity and high sugar levels to create
a fully-flavoured soup. The best onions are Rose de Roscoff.
Spanish onions, although lacking in acidity, will also work.
If you like a strong onion flavour, caramelise the onions for a
further 15 minutes, until very dark brown.

By quickly boiling the wine you are removing most of the
alcohol, which has a bitterness, but keeping all the fruity
qualities and acidity of the wine.

Variation

You could replace the water with a brown chicken stock
(see page 280) for a richer soup.

STUFFED BRAISED ONION

The Rose de Roscoff onion is probably one of the world's best onions, this according to both my British *and* French friends, and has a whole glorious heritage behind it, having been grown in Brittany since the seventeenth century. It is synonymous with excellence and the wonderful image of the Onion Johnnies invading Britain on their bicycles, their Calvados flasks tied to their handlebars to keep them fired up.

This recipe is actually three recipes in one: three different stuffings for this beautiful onion. You can either follow the main recipe for the simple, rustic pork and sage stuffing or choose one of the alternative options overleaf. The onions are served with a creamy soubise sauce for which I've used English white onions as they are sweeter and softer than the Roscoff; they will cook more easily and will provide a lovely foil to the savoury stuffings.

SERVES 4

Preparation time: 30 minutes
Cooking time: 1½ hours

For the braised onion
4 Rose de Roscoff onions (about 190g each)
250ml water or light chicken stock
50g unsalted butter
2 thyme sprigs
1 garlic clove, crushed
3 pinches sea salt
2 black peppercorns

For the pork stuffing
150g sausage meat, coarse textured
50g wholemeal breadcrumbs
1 medium egg
3 sage leaves
4 pinches freshly ground black pepper
pinch sea salt

To braise the onions, peel each onion, ensuring you leave the base of the root still attached – it will form the base of the braised onion and give it support to hold its shape. Remove the first tough outside layer.

Slice the top from each onion one quarter of the way down, leaving three quarters of the onion and the base. Reserve the tops for the soubise sauce. Place the onions in a medium saucepan. Add enough water or stock to come halfway up the onions. Add the butter, thyme, garlic and the seasoning. Bring to a boil, then turn down to a gentle simmer for 1 hour, covered with a lid. Carefully lift out the onions on to a tray to cool, and reserve the cooking liquor.

Once the onions have cooled to just warm, use a teaspoon to scoop out the centre of each to create a receptacle, leaving three outer layers to give the onion stability once stuffed. Reserve the centres for the pork stuffing and soubise sauce.

Preheat the oven to 100°C/Gas Mark ¼.

To make the pork stuffing, in a large bowl, mix all of the ingredients. With a spoon, stuff each onion and transfer to a small roasting tin. Pour a quarter of the reserved onion cooking liquor into the tin and bake in the oven for 18 minutes – check the centre of the stuffing with a probe, it must reach a core temperature of 80°C; if not return to the oven for a few minutes.

Continued overleaf →

For the soubise sauce

40g unsalted butter

300g white onions, chopped

2 garlic cloves, sliced

2 pinches sea salt

100g double cream

grating of nutmeg

pinch cayenne pepper

lemon juice, to taste

For the soubise sauce, in a medium heavy-based saucepan on a low heat, place the butter, chopped onions, the reserved tops and centres from the braised onions, the garlic and salt and sweat for 15 minutes with the lid on. Remove the lid and cook for a further 10 minutes to evaporate some of the cooking liquid. You'll end up with a little over a tablespoon of liquid. Transfer the onions and cooking liquid to a blender and purée until smooth. Return to the saucepan, add the cream and simmer for a few minutes. Taste and adjust the seasoning. Add a grating of nutmeg, the cayenne pepper, and a dash of lemon juice, if necessary. Taste again.

To serve, place a spoonful of the soubise sauce in the centre of each plate with one of the stuffed onions on top.

Stuffed braised onions with Jerusalem artichoke

For the Jerusalem artichoke stuffing

200g Jerusalem artichokes, peeled and cut into 1cm dice

100g Agata or Estima potatoes, peeled and diced

20g unsalted butter

½ garlic clove, puréed

pinch sea salt

pinch freshly ground black pepper

To serve

10g black truffle, chopped

Preheat the oven to 180°C/Gas Mark 4.

To make the stuffing, cook the Jerusalem artichokes in boiling water for 4 minutes, drain and reserve. Cook the potatoes in boiling water for 7 minutes. Drain in a colander then place in a bowl. Crush the potatoes with a fork. Stir in the butter, garlic, salt, pepper and Jerusalem artichoke.

With a spoon, stuff each onion and transfer to a small roasting tin. Pour a quarter of the reserved onion cooking liquor into the tin and bake in the oven for 2–3 minutes.

To serve, grate or slice your precious summer truffle and sprinkle or lay on top. Serve as for the main recipe, with the onion soubise sauce.

Stuffed braised onions with salted cod

For the salted cod

1 garlic clove, finely sliced

½ thyme sprig

½ bay leaf, torn into 4

3 basil leaves

1 tsp coarse rock salt

½ tsp finely grated lemon zest

150g cod fillet, skinned, filleted and pin-boned

4 tsp extra virgin olive oil, plus a little extra for drizzling

For the brandade

200g Agata or Estima potatoes, peeled and diced

50ml olive oil

150g Salted Cod

½ garlic clove, puréed

squeeze of lemon juice

2 pinches cayenne pepper

For the topping

50g Comté cheese, finely grated

To serve

10g onion seeds, toasted

Preheat the oven to 100°C/Gas Mark ¼.

For the salted cod, in a pestle and mortar grind all the seasonings and herbs together. Line a tray with cling film, lay the fish on top, sprinkle over the cure and roll the fish in the mixture, pressing firmly so it sticks to the fish. Tightly wrap in cling film and leave to marinate in the fridge for 6 hours.

Wash off the marinade under running cold water, pat the fish dry with a cloth and lay on a small non-stick oven tray. Brush with the olive oil and put in the oven for 8–10 minutes, until the fish is barely cooked. Cool down a little and break the flesh into beautiful petals. The flesh will be shiny and snow white. Drizzle with more olive oil and reserve. Once cool, lift the cod on to a small tray.

Increase the oven setting to 180°C/Gas Mark 4.

For the brandade, cook the potatoes in boiling water for 7 minutes. Drain in a colander then place in a bowl. Crush the potatoes with a fork and stir in the olive oil. Fold in the fish, garlic, lemon juice and cayenne pepper. Taste and correct the seasoning if necessary.

With a spoon, stuff each onion with the brandade and sprinkle the Comté cheese over the top. Transfer to a small roasting tin. Pour a quarter of the onion cooking liquor into the tin and bake in the oven for 2–3 minutes.

Serve as for the main recipe, with the onion soubise sauce and the onions seeds sprinkled over the top.

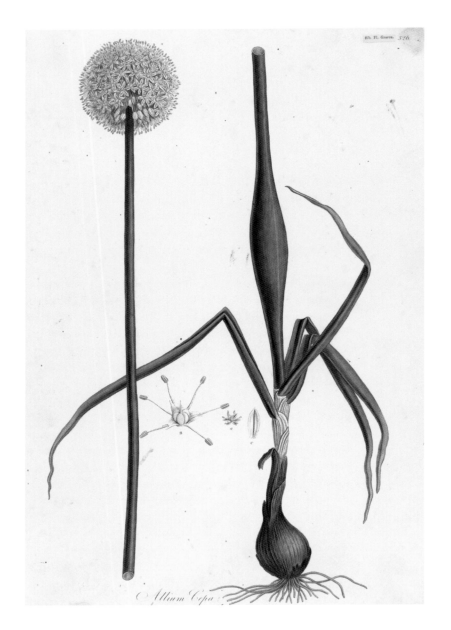

Allium Cepa

Left: The onion plant, Allium cepa, *depicted in* Flora Graeca, *vol. 4: t.326 (1823). The first six volumes of the work by John Sibthorp (1758–96), Sherardian Professor of Botany at Oxford University (the Chair endowed by leading botanist William Sherard, 1659–1728,) were published posthumously by J. E. Smith. This followed the death of Sibthorp during one of his botanical tours of Europe, this time to Greece, gathering material for* Flora Graeca.

BEETROOT

IF EVER THERE WERE A VEGETABLE that has been 'reinvented' in the last few decades it is the beetroot. Once consigned to memories of teatime salad with grandma: lettuce, tomato, boiled egg, a slice of ham and thick wedges of vinegary red beetroot from a jar, staining everything on the plate pink, it has become the darling of the contemporary kitchen, celebrated for its natural sweetness and its many heritage hues: golden, white, deep purple, candy-striped...

Early examples of the beet family, including sugar beet, tended to be parsnip shaped. It wasn't until the sixteenth century that the more familiar round beetroot became fashionable.

Natural sugar is a characteristic of the beet family – after all the sugar beet, whose roots are creamy and shaped like a parsnip, is grown specifically to provide beet sugar. In the seventeenth century, a soil scientist named Olivier de Serres first discovered that a sweet syrup could be made from the root; and in 1747 the German scientist, Andreas Sigismund Marggraf, developed the process of boiling up the juices and water into a syrup until crystallisation occurs, on which sugar beet production is still based. These days over half the sugar used in the UK comes from sugar beet, as opposed to sugar cane.

Most cultivated varieties of beet have evolved from the wild sea beet that is native to the coastlines of Europe, Asia, North Africa and the Middle East since prehistoric times, and is still a favourite with foragers. The Greeks and Romans cultivated a form of leaf beet (similar to chard), however the Greeks were only interested in the leaves for medicinal purposes and gave offerings of leaf beets to Apollo, the sun god. The Romans, however, appear to have used both root and leaf as a curative and as a food.

The leaves continued to be the main attraction until the middle of the sixteenth century when the round red beetroot we know today began to be cultivated in Germany and its popularity spread through Europe. John Gerard wrote in his *The Herball*, of 'the red and beautiful root (which is preferred before the leaves, as well in beauty as in goodness).'

Beetroot really took off in Britain in Victorian times. Mrs Beeton noted that the cooked leaves were a substitute for spinach, and the root also 'may be prepared in several ways, but its most general use is in salad'. These days, nutritionists echo the wisdom of the ancients in recognising the health benefits of beetroot. The leaves are rich in calcium, provitamin A and vitamin C and the roots are a source of folic acid, fibre, iron and potassium, while both leaves and roots are a good source of magnesium and vitamin B_6. Studies show that beetroot may be important in cardiovascular health, and it is suggested that drinking beetroot juice may benefit endurance athletes, thanks to its naturally occurring nitrates, which can help increase the blood flow to the muscles.

'I like the idea that the beetroot soup, borscht, could be the equivalent of the healing chicken soup which every Jewish mother prescribes,' says

Raymond. 'My partner, whose mum is Russian, makes it at least once a week – it is probably the secret of my youthfulness!'

In terms of flavour, he notes that amongst the many varieties 'some are quite flat-tasting; some are too woody and almost unpleasantly earthy; some are overly-sweet. The best are packed with flavour and have the right balance of that characteristic earthiness and the sweetness that develops slowly over time, which is why I would say that a mature beetroot will have a bigger flavour than a baby one. I have tasted some big beetroot with an extraordinarily complex flavour.'

At Kew the varieties grown include Cheltenham Green Top, an old variety from 1883, which is very sweet and tender. It is red, but paler than many varieties, and long – shaped like a parsnip – a reminder of the beetroot of ancient times. There is also Rouge Crapaudine, the oldest beetroot in cultivation, dating back to Charlemagne's time in the eighth century, which has an almost black skin, cracked and creviced, like bark.

'My favourites,' says Raymond, 'are Chioggia, with its pink and white ringed flesh – which has quite a complex flavour; Golden, which is a heritage variety that dates back to 1806 and was considered a delicacy in Victorian times as a change to red beetroot; and Bull's Blood, which is a very good heritage beetroot.

There is also an Italian beetroot that I dream of: yellow and weighing about half a kilogram. We grew it once in the vegetable garden of my restaurant and then the name was lost and we haven't found it since. But I remember its perfect balance of flavour, and I will go on searching. One day I will find that beetroot!'

Opposite: A member of the beet family, Beta vulgaris *from Joseph Jacob Plenck's* Icones Plantarum Medicinalium, *vol. 2: t.169 (1788–1812)*

Tab. 169.

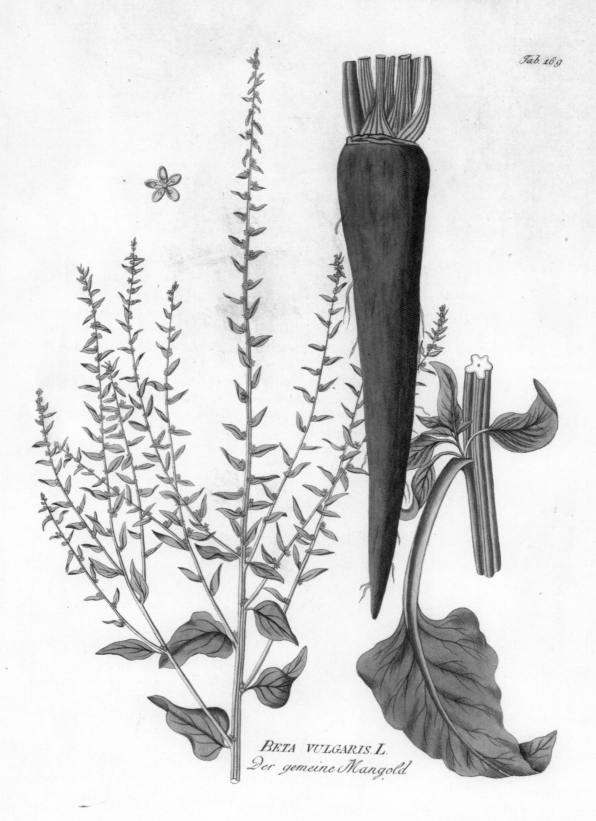

BETA VULGARIS. L.
Der gemeine Mangold

GROWING NOTES

Sow from March to July in well-drained soil around every 3–4 weeks if you want to harvest beetroot of a similar size through to October.

Dig some well-rotted manure or compost into the bed the autumn before planting.

Sow in shallow drills (furrows), about 3cm deep, one seed every 5cm, cover with soil and water in well. If planting more than one drill, leave a space of 30cm between each one. Thin out the seedlings when they are about 2.5cm tall, leaving around 10cm between each remaining one to give enough space for the roots (the beetroot) to develop and ensure that the nutrients in the soil aren't overstretched in trying to support too many roots. You can eat the seedlings that you have pulled up in salads.

Beetroot seeds can also be sown and thinned out in a similar way in large pots on a patio. Alternatively, to give the plants a head start, you can sow the seeds indoors in modules – three to a module. Don't thin them out, once established just plant each group of seedlings 30cm apart and they will grow on in clumps.

Keep weedfree and water in dry periods. Keeping the soil moist can stop the plants from bolting, i.e. putting their energies into growing flowers and seeds, rather than the roots.

You can harvest any time from June to October, once the beetroot have reached golf-ball size (around eight weeks after sowing, depending on the variety). Slightly larger ones will take about 12 weeks, and if you like your beetroot to be quite big in the more traditional fashion, you can happily leave them in for a few more weeks.

Dig up the beetroot with a garden fork and twist off the stems, then you can store them until around mid-spring in the cool and dark of a cellar or garage in boxes of sand or light soil.

Right: The leaves of the growing beetroot show a diversity of colour in the beds at Kew.

RAYMOND'S FLAVOUR NOTES

I love the magnificent Chioggia, with its white flesh and pink concentric rings, and the wine-red heritage variety, Bull's blood.

My mum used to make a warm beetroot salad with just salt and pepper, a dash of olive oil and vinegar. It was stunning just as it was, but you could crumble over some feta, ewe's cheese or mozzarella.

To cook beetroot for salad, I would scrub it well, so that you don't pass on its earthy flavour to the water, then simmer it until tender. That way you keep in as much moisture as possible. If you roast beetroot, you intensify its flavour, but you also lose around 20 per cent of its moisture.

And, of course, you can grate it raw into salads, which is delicious, and also add the young leaves. Even the older leaves needn't be wasted. You can chop them up and add them to a vegetable soup.

BEEF TARTARE AND PICKLED BEETROOT

I would like to apologise for the very cheffy presentation. Adam and Ben, my development chefs, are passionate and got carried away with their creativity and with the extraordinary colours and textures of the garden in autumn. They get full marks for pairing pickled beetroot with tartare, though - it's perfect!

SERVES 4

Preparation time: 50 minutes

For the tartare
300g beef fillet, cut into 5mm dice
30g banana shallot, finely chopped
3 flat-leaf parsley sprigs, finely
   chopped
30g capers, roughly chopped
30g gherkins, roughly chopped
2 tsp Dijon mustard
5 drops hot pepper sauce
10 drops Worcestershire sauce
2 pinches sea salt

For the beetroot garnish
1 baby Golden beetroot, peeled
1 baby Chioggia beetroot, peeled
1 tbsp extra virgin olive oil
1 tbsp white wine vinegar
pinch caster sugar
pinch sea salt
pinch freshly ground white pepper
1 cooked ruby beetroot

For the horseradish cream
130g creamed horseradish
90g crème fraîche
4g sea salt
pinch caster sugar
1 tsp lemon juice
cayenne pepper, to taste

To serve
micro leaves or young salad leaves

To prepare the tartare, in a large mixing bowl, stir together all the ingredients, taste and adjust the seasoning as required.

For the beetroot garnish, finely slice the Golden and Chioggia beetroot and place in separate bowls. Mix the oil, vinegar, sugar and seasoning with a tablespoon of water. Add half the mixture to the Golden beetroot and leave to pickle for 10 minutes. Taste and correct the seasoning if required. Repeat for the Chioggia beetroot. Cut the ruby beetroot into 1cm dice and reserve.

For the horseradish cream, stir all the ingredients together, or, for a smoother texture, place all the ingredients in a blender and purée until smooth. Taste and adjust the seasoning if necessary.

To serve, place a 12cm ring in the centre of a serving plate, spread a quarter of the tartare mix evenly inside it, smooth the top with a palette knife, and repeat this for the remaining three plates. Drain the pickled beetroot on a piece of kitchen paper, then arrange beautifully on top of each serving of beef tartare at the same time as the diced cooked ruby beetroot. Pipe or spoon a few little mounds of horseradish cream on top. Finish the dish with a few micro leaves or young salad leaves.

Chef's note
We are lucky to have an extraordinary range of beetroot varieties at Kew but you can, of course use any you have.

Variations
This tartare can be made with tuna, salmon or many other fish.

You could serve the tartare more simply with a salad of raw and cooked beetroot or a herby garden salad. It is even better with toasted sourdough bread or traditional French fries.

GARDEN BEETROOT AND ROSCOFF ONION TART

Working in the gardens of Kew, having sown our seed in the rich soil, we tended the young plants with sunlight and water. We took these plants to perfect maturity, and as a chef you cannot ask for more. In this delicious starter the beetroot is cooked from raw, rather than being blanched first, which concentrates its wonderful earthy flavour.

To ensure the success of this dish it is crucial to cover the beetroot with the circle of paper secured by a ring in order to keep all the moisture and the flavour.

SERVES 2

Preparation time: 10 minutes, plus chilling
Cooking time: 40 minutes
You will also need: 2 x 12cm ovenproof blini pans; 2 x 11cm metal rings

For the pastry base
300g ready-rolled puff pastry, chilled then rolled to 3mm

For the beetroot
300g (about 6 small) Golden or Chioggia beetroot, scrubbed clean
pinch sea salt
2 pinches black pepper
20g unsalted butter, warm

For the pastry base, line a baking sheet with greaseproof paper. Cut the pastry into two 13cm discs using a ring or small plate and place on the lined baking sheet. Transfer to the fridge, or ideally the freezer, for at least 1 hour, to prevent the pastry being sticky.

Preheat the oven to 180°C/Gas Mark 4.

To prepare the beetroot, cut the root off each one. Using a mandolin set to a thickness of 1mm, slice into thin discs and transfer to a bowl. Season with salt and pepper. Stir in the warm butter to ensure each slice of beetroot is evenly coated.

To cook the beetroot, place a 9cm metal ring in a 12cm blini pan. Layer the seasoned beetroot discs inside the ring in an even rosace pattern three layers deep. The metal ring will facilitate the building of the beetroot and keep it upright and in a perfect circle. Repeat this with the other blini pan and metal ring. Cut a circle of greaseproof paper to the same size as the blini pan. Lift the metal ring off the beetroot and lay the greaseproof paper on top of the beetroot rosace, then press the ring back over the rosace. By placing the ring over the paper you will trap the steam trying to escape, which will keep the beetroot beautifully moist. Cook the beetroot rosaces on a medium heat for 2 minutes, until the sides start to bubble. Some juices from the beetroot will boil in the pan – this is important as it speeds up the cooking of the beetroot in the oven and gives a nice light caramelisation to the beetroot.

Continued overleaf $\rightarrow$

For the onion jam

10g unsalted butter

200g Rose de Roscoff onion
(about 1), sliced

pinch sea salt

pinch black pepper

10ml Jerez vinegar

To build the tarts

1 egg yolk, beaten with 2 tsp
water for an egg wash

pinch black pepper

1 tsp orange and thyme dried
powder (optional; orange zest
and thyme dried in the oven
at 100°C/Gas Mark ¼ for
1 hour, then blitzed to a powder)

For the Jerez vinaigrette

4 tsp Jerez vinegar, boiled for
30 seconds

40ml good-quality olive oil

pinch sea salt

pinch black pepper

To serve

150g mixed salad leaves

60g cottage cheese

Transfer the beetroot to the oven for 10–12 minutes. Remove from the oven, leave to rest and cool completely. Lift off the rings and greaseproof paper from the cooled beetroot rosaces and turn them out on to a small plate (the coloured side, with its golden rosace pattern will be facing upwards). Set aside.

For the onion jam, in a medium saucepan on a medium heat, melt the butter and add the onion with the salt and pepper. Cook for 35–40 minutes, covered with a lid, until softened but not caramelised. Stir every 5 minutes to prevent the onions from burning. Deglaze the pan with the vinegar, scraping any browned bits from the bottom with a wooden spoon, and boil for 20 seconds. Taste and adjust the seasoning if necessary. Leave to cool completely.

To build and cook the beetroot tarts, divide the onion jam equally between the two pastry discs and with the back of a spoon spread the onions to a thin layer leaving a gap of 1cm around the edge . Lightly brush the pastry edges with a thin coating of egg wash and sprinkle them with the black pepper and powdered orange and thyme, if using. Using a palette knife, lift each golden rosace right into the centre of each pastry base. Place a piece of greaseproof paper over each of the tarts and place a cooling rack on top of them. Transfer to the oven for 20 minutes, until the sides of the pastry are golden brown. The parchment paper and cooling rack on the tarts help keep the moisture in the beetroot; it will also ensure the pastry rises evenly and the beetroot slices do not curl whilst cooking.

Make the Jerez vinaigrette. Mix all the ingredients, taste and adjust the seasoning if necessary.

To serve, dress the leaves with half the vinaigrette and arrange on each plate. Scatter the cottage cheese over the salad. Brush the remaining vinaigrette over the beetroot tarts to give flavour and a beautiful glaze and serve on each plate.

Chef's note

Once the beetroot has been cut or sliced, use within 20 minutes to prevent discolouration or oxidation.

APPLES

'ABOUT 25 YEARS AGO I took part in a tasting of heritage English apples with the Royal Horticultural Society, and among them was the Queen Cox,' says Raymond. 'Tasting that apple was one of those experiences that I will always remember: it had such a complexity and length of flavour, of sweetness and acidity, a lovely light texture, juiciness and perfume. When I fall in love, I fall in love! I decided then and there that one day I would have an orchard alongside my restaurant that would celebrate all the regions of Great Britain and some varieties from France as well. So, now we are growing around 400 old varieties of fruit trees, including around 100 apple trees, some of which come from tiny villages and have beautiful names and lovely stories behind them. I was determined to do it, because when I arrived in Britain I was shocked at how many orchards had atrophied, and how many of the old apple varieties had been almost lost.'

We think of the apple orchard as quintessentially English yet the apple we enjoy today is descended from the wild fruit grown across Kazakhstan and parts of China.

In the 1970s orchards all around the country were 'grubbed up' when grain subsidies from the EU meant other crops such as wheat were more lucrative to grow than apples, and less labour intensive. As a result the sad reality is that Britain's orchard acreage has been eroded to a quarter of what it was in 1950.

Of course, we think of the apple orchard – particularly where cider apple varieties are concerned – as something quintessentially English (in Victorian times cider was such a favourite drink that farm labourers were often part-paid in cider, until the practice was outlawed in 1887). Yet DNA evidence shows that the apple as we know it today is descended from a wild apple grown in the mountains that stretch across Kazakhstan and parts of China. It is an icy habitat, which explains why the apple needs freezing or near-freezing conditions to ensure successful germination; and why you generally won't find apple orchards in hot climates.

The Romans brought the Kazakhstan apple to Britain, where it cross-pollinated with the native British crab apple, and according to a study of DNA carried out in 2012, many modern apples are more closely related to the crab apple than to the original Far Eastern apple. And talking of DNA, in another study two years earlier, scientists finished decoding the complete genome of a Golden Delicious apple, which showed that it has around 57,000 genes, almost twice as many as a human being.

Thousands of different apple varieties are known: some 7,500 the world over and nearly 3,000 in Britain. The National Fruit Collection, held at Brogdale farm in Kent, contains over 2,000 different apples, and yet, in our supermarkets until fairly recently our choice was reduced to only a handful. 'And the reason?' asks Raymond. 'The popularity of one single apple: the subject of that genome study, the Golden Delicious. If an apple can be intelligent, then it was a very clever apple: engineered to be good

Britain is home to nearly 3,000 apple varieties, many of which have been grown locally for centuries, and have wonderful characterful flavours.

to eat and cook, to bake well, to make good purée, to have a good colour and a big yield, and to be resistant to disease. But it is not an interesting apple. Sweetness has been the defining factor in the fruit market, when it should not be. True flavour is all about complexity and the contrast of sweetness and acidity that you find in apples like the Queen Cox, Cox's Orange Pippin, Egremont Russet and Chivers Delight. These have real, characterful, amazing flavours when you bite into them. Happily, we are beginning to rediscover and value more and more of these distinctive old varieties. I would especially love to see the whole Cox family regularly on supermarket shelves. They may be small, but they have everything else going for them.'

For the garden at Kew, Raymond worked with William Sibley of the East Malling Trust. Since the original East Malling Research station was set up a century ago, around 85 per cent of the world's apples have originated there. Space is at a premium at Kew, so Alice and Joe, under William's direction, have trained varieties such as Blenheim Orange, Adam's Pearmain, Lord Lambourne and Egremont Russet in espalier and step-over forms (see pages 206–7), so that they create attractive borders around other fruit and vegetable beds and their fruit production can be maximised.

The apple that is the most nostalgic for Raymond is the Reine de Reinette as it was the one he grew up with in France. 'I remember it was golden-brownish in colour, a bit like an Egremont Russet. My mother used it to make the most simple but extraordinary apple tart. She would roll out some shortcrust pastry, slice the apple straight on to it in overlapping concentric circles and add a tiny bit of butter and sugar. It would go in the oven until the apples became fluffy and caramelised and then she would finish it by pouring over a beautiful custard and returning it to the oven. I can still remember the smell of it filling the house as it baked. It is a recipe that is so simple and so beautiful that I constantly want to share it.'

Opposite (above and below): Apples and other fruit trees such as pear and quince lend themselves to training over framework and against fences and walls, so can be incorporated into small spaces.

AN APPLE IN THE KITCHEN

Raymond's favourites for...

★ Best for | ✣ Best all-rounders

STEWING/ PUREE

Blenheim Orange ★

Adam's Pearmain ★

Cox's Orange Pippin ✣

Queen Cox

Devonshire Quarrenden

BAKING

Cox's Orange Pippin ✣

Adam's Pearmain ★

Annie Elizabeth

D'Arcy Spice

TARTS

Chivers Delight ★

Captain Kidd ★

Adam's Pearmain

Blenheim Orange

Cox's Orange Pippin ✣

D'Arcy Spice

Devonshire Quarrenden

Discovery

Egremont Russet

Lord Lambourne

TARTE TATIN

Captain Kidd ★

Chivers Delight ★

Devonshire Quarrenden

Queen Cox

Braeburn

Granny Smith

JUICE

Egremont Russet ★

Cox's Orange Pippin ✦

Captain Kidd

Chivers Delight

GROWING NOTES

If you are buying several trees it is more economical to buy one-year-old bare-rooted trees, and also, if you are training them into shapes it is easier to manipulate younger branches. The roots will need to be soaked in water and then planted as soon as possible, however in the first year after planting you will only get a bare minimum of fruit, and will need to take the apples off as soon you see them starting to form (i.e. they will be too small to eat). Otherwise they will weigh too heavily on the immature branches, and may bend them out of shape, or even break them. In the following year you should get a small harvest.

If you want fruit straight away, you can also buy two-year old trees, which will bear some fruit in the first autumn. Small varieties can be grown in containers and, as at Kew, espalier and step-over trees (see opposite) can be grown against a fence, wall or framework.

Choose a sunny, sheltered position. When planting, if the tree needs staking, put in the stake at the same time as planting, to avoid damaging the root ball by driving it in later. You can top-dress with a sprinkling of Soil Association-certified organic chicken manure pellets and mulch with a layer of compost.

Some apples are self-fertile (nurseries sell a special clone of Queen Cox), but most trees need to be pollinated from a different cultivar that flowers at the same time, allowing bees to do their work (trees pollinated in this way generally produce a better crop). The pollinator doesn't have to be in your own garden, it could be a neighbour's tree. Apple trees are classed in 'pollination groups' according to their flowering time, which, if you want to buy several different trees, makes the task of choosing easier. A few combinations don't work, for example Cox's Orange Pippin and Kidd's Orange Red (which has the characteristics of an English Cox, but was developed in New Zealand) are incompatible in terms of pollination – so it is best to seek advice when you buy your trees. One easy answer is to buy a 'family tree', which has two or three different varieties grafted on one tree. However these can sometimes be difficult to prune, as each tends to grow at a different rate.

The art of the trained and shaped espalier tree was perfected by Jean-Baptiste de la Quintinye, director of Louis XIV's kitchen gardens at the Palace of Versailles, for practical as well as aesthetic reasons. Not only do espalier trees look good against a wall or fence, they also save space and can result in increased production. In a large apple tree branches naturally grow towards the sun, and as the tree grows bushier, the inner branches can get crowded out from the light and fruit may not form or ripen so well. However, with an espalier tree, only one dominant branch is trained upwards against a wall, fence or structure, and the lower ones are trained and secured outwards on either side, so that the tree is 'flattened'. Since the branches can no longer focus their energies on trying to reach upwards, the outstretched branches concentrate instead on producing blossom, and consequently fruit. This fruit in turn benefits from greater exposure to the sun and the increased air circulation helps keep disease at bay.

Step-over trees are very low-growing – i.e. they are literally small enough to step over – and can be used to edge or divide a kitchen garden. 'The technique of training them does require patience,' admits Alice. 'First we put in a series of posts at intervals, and secured a wire across the top of them. We planted the trees in front of the posts, about 1.2m apart. As the trees grew, we took the lead branch of each one and tied it to a cane. This acts like a splint to keep the branch from breaking. Then we bent each branch (plus cane) gently downwards (each branch needs to be bent in the same direction) and tied it to the wire. The idea is that gradually, over the whole season, you keep lowering each branch (still tied to its cane) by about 20–30° at a time, securing it to the wire as you go, until eventually each one becomes horizontal and you have created a continuous "fence". In summer you can prune any side branches back to three leaves to help produce plenty of fruit in the autumn.'

Top and above left: step-over and espalier trees are practical as well as attractive. The outstretched branches, secured against a fence, framework or wall, are better exposed to sunlight than those of a bushy tree. This allows them to concentrate their energy on producing a profusion of blossom (above right) and consequently, plenty of fruit.

RAYMOND'S FLAVOUR NOTES

In France, we have always known that there are certain apples that are better for baking, juicing, purées or tarts, whereas in Britain they tend to be defined as 'for cooking' or 'for eating'. But since I dreamed of my own orchard I have tasted hundreds and hundreds of apples, and kept charts of their flavours and behaviours when cooked in certain ways.

When it comes to purée, the apple that I have struggled to come to terms with is the Bramley. I had never tasted one before I came to England. I knew that the British had a great affection for it, but I found there was nothing I could love about that apple. Yes, it breaks down and purées very quickly – of course it does, because it is loose-fibred and full of water and acidity – but that means that you have to compensate for its sourness by adding lots of sugar. I don't understand the attraction. In our tasting sessions I found many more apples that I preferred for purée, such as Blenheim Orange (an Oxfordshire apple from 1740); Adam's Pearmain (an early nineteenth-century apple from Norfolk and Hereford); Queen Cox (a Berkshire variety from 1953); the older Cox's Orange Pippin (1825), of which Queen Cox is a clone; and Devonshire Quarrenden, a really old apple from Devon that goes back to 1678.

For baking, I like Cox's Orange Pippin, Adam's Pearmain, Annie Elizabeth (a nineteenth-century apple from Leicester) and d'Arcy Spice (an Essex variety from 1785).

For tarts, I would recommend Chivers Delight, Captain Kidd, Adam's Pearmain; Blenheim Orange; Devonshire Quarrenden; Egremont Russet from Somerset (1872); and Lord Lambourne from Bedfordshire (1907). What you are looking for is an apple that you can slice about half a centimetre thick, that will fluff up but still hold its texture and won't disintegrate into a purée. It needs a high enough level of acidity and sugar to keep a lively, characterful flavour through the cooking process. Captain Kidd is also excellent for tarte Tatin.

For juice, Egremont Russet is my favourite, because it has a lovely layering of richness and acidity.

Apples are rich in provitamin A and vitamin C, and since the provitamin A is most concentrated in the skin, and the vitamin C – like potatoes – is found just under the skin, it is good to leave the skins on when you can.

I have also found a lovely way to use crab apples. I poach them in sugar syrup – made with 50 per cent sugar to water – leaving their little stalks on, and the poached crab apples will keep in sterilised jars for about a year: very pretty.

Opposite: Kirke's Scarlet Admirable Apple (a variety of Malus domestica) *as illustrated by botanical artist E.D. Smith in* Flora and Pomona *(pl. 10), a work by horticulturalist and gardener to the aristocracy, Charles McIntosh (1794–1864) .*

E.D. Smith delin.

S. Watts sculp!

London: Published by Thomas Kelly, 17, Paternoster Row. 1830.

APPLE AND WATERCRESS SALAD

The watercress season spans a large period of the year in the UK, running from April to October. In spring, the young leaves are crisp and tender, while in autumn they have developed a wonderful peppery flavour. For me the spicy autumn watercress is best in this salad, teamed with the first of the autumn apples, but you could also make it in spring, with apples that you have stored over the winter.

SERVES 4

Preparation time: 15 minutes
Cooking time: 10 minutes

For the watercress dressing
250g watercress leaves
30g flat-leaf parsley, leaves picked
4 tbsp extra virgin olive oil
4 tbsp hazelnut oil
30g ice cubes
sea salt and freshly ground black
    pepper

For the apple purée
2 large Braeburn apples, peeled,
    cored and cut into small dice
50ml water
dash of lemon juice
pinch caster sugar (optional)

For the watercress salad
1 tbsp extra virgin olive oil
2 tsp lemon juice
2 tsp water
2 pinches sea salt
2 pinches caster sugar
240g watercress leaves, large
    stalks removed

To serve
2 Braeburn apples
50g hazelnuts, toasted and chopped
1 shallot, sliced into rings, washed
    under cold water for 2 minutes

For the watercress dressing, blanch the watercress and parsley in boiling water for 30 seconds to remove some of the bitterness, then refresh in iced water. Place in a large colander and squeeze out as much water as possible.

Chop then transfer to a blender with the two oils and blend on full speed, until completely smooth. Add the ice cubes and continue to blend to loosen the dressing; the cold from the ice will also ensure that it does not lose its vibrant colour. Taste and correct the seasoning with salt and pepper if necessary. Pass through a fine sieve and reserve in the fridge.

For the apple purée, in a medium saucepan on a medium heat, cook the apples with the water and lemon juice for 10 minutes with a lid on. Purée in a blender, taste and add a pinch of sugar or dash more lemon juice if necessary. Pass through a fine sieve and reserve in the fridge.

For the watercress salad, in a large bowl, mix the oil, lemon juice, water, salt and sugar. Taste and correct the seasoning, then toss with the watercress.

To serve, spread the apple purée on each serving plate. Core and chop the apples into wedges and scatter pieces around the plates. Place the dressed watercress salad in the centre and drizzle over the watercress dressing. Finish with the chopped nuts and shallot rings.

HAM HOCK AND APPLE TERRINE

My mum would always cook with a pressure cooker and I have brilliant memories of wonderful stews being concocted in them. They may be regarded as old-fashioned but I think they're fantastic and I use one to cook the ham hock for this terrine. Cooking under pressure means you can reduce the amount of liquid needed to cover the food; you retain more of its water-soluble nutrients and, in this case, the texture, flavour and succulent moisture in the ham. Cooking this way is about 70 per cent faster than cooking on a stove, so you've also reduced your energy costs and time. For those of you that haven't yet discovered the magic of this type of cooking, I've given instructions for cooking the ham on the stove (see page 215). The apples and apple juice not only lighten this terrine, they enhance its character.

SERVES 6–8 (FROM 1 TERRINE)

Preparation time: overnight
Cooking time: 1½ hours
You will also need: pressure
    cooker (optional; see Cook's
    note); 18 x 11 x 4cm plastic
    container for the terrine, plus
    one extra for pressing (see
    Cook's note)

For the ham hock

1.5kg ham hock (1 large or 2 small)
1 pig's trotter, sliced down the
    length (optional; it will add
    flavour and natural
    gelatine)
1.5 litres cold water
500ml fresh apple juice
100g celery (about 2 sticks),
    cut in half widthways
100g white onion (about 1),
    cut into 6
1 bouquet garni (2 bay leaves,
    5g parsley, 2g thyme)
8 black peppercorns
1.5 gelatine leaves
30ml white wine vinegar

To cook the ham hock, place the ham hock and pig's trotter in a pressure cooker, cover with the cold water and bring to the boil for 1 minute. Skim to remove the impurities and albumens, which will rise to the surface. Turn down to a gentle simmer, add the apple juice, celery, onion, bouquet garni and black peppercorns, cover with the lid, return to the heat and bring back to the boil. When the pressure pin rises on the lid and the steam is released, turn the valve to setting 1 and turn the heat down to the lowest setting.

Cook for 1½ hours, then turn off the heat, release the pressure valve and leave the pan to depressurise – the steam escaping will create a bit of noise – don't panic, it needs to escape; the pressure pin will drop down completely and the steam will have escaped, then it is safe to open the lid again.

Using a slotted spoon, lift out the ham on to a large plate or tray, then remove the vegetables and discard. Taste and correct the seasoning of the cooking stock, then strain through a fine sieve and reserve – this will become the base of the jelly.

Soften the gelatine in cold water. Once soft, measure out 150ml of the strained cooking stock, which is what you will need to set the terrine. Stir in the gelatine along with the white wine vinegar and mix well.

When the ham hock has cooled for 20 minutes, peel the rind and fat and discard (see Cook's note). Flake the meat. No additional seasoning should be necessary as the hock will have natural seasoning from its cure.

Continued overleaf $\longrightarrow$

To finish the terrine

35g flat-leaf parsley, blanched for
  15 seconds and roughly
  chopped
1 Cox's Orange Pippin apple, cut
  into 5mm dice
50g baby capers, washed and
  patted dry

For the apple purée

2 Blenheim Orange apples, peeled,
  cored and chopped
100ml fresh organic apple juice
caster sugar (optional)
juice of ¼ lemon (optional)

To serve

1 Cox's Orange Pippin apple,
  diced and sliced
1 banana shallot, sliced into thin
  rings and washed under cold
  water for 2 minutes
olive oil, for dressing
micro leaves (optional)
freshly toasted pain de campagne
  (optional)

To finish the terrine mixture, mix the chopped parsley, apple dice and capers with the meat.

To build the terrine, line the insides of the mould with 2 layers of cling film, ensuring that you have a 10cm overhang on each side and end of the mould to enable you to wrap the terrine neatly and prevent any discolouration.

Fill the terrine with the meat and apple mixture, pour in the 150ml of warm cooking liquor and lightly press so a thin layer of liquor covers the meat. Gently fold the overhanging cling film to cover the terrine, place the second plastic container on top and fill it with 1kg of weight to compress the terrine (you could use some tins of beans, for example). Leave for 12 hours or overnight.

For the apple purée, in a medium saucepan on a medium heat, cook the apples and apple juice for 5 minutes with a lid on, stirring every 2 minutes to avoid the apples catching on the bottom of the pan. Remove from the heat and pour into a blender. Blend for 1 minute on full speed until you have a smooth purée. Pour into a bowl and leave to cool. Depending on the sweetness or acidity of the apple, you may need to balance the purée with a little sugar or lemon juice.

To serve, remove the terrine from the mould and unwrap the cling film. Then, to make slicing easier, re-wrap it tightly in two fresh layers of cling film. This might seem excessive, but the cling film will give the terrine the support it needs to stop it from falling to pieces as you cut into it. Slice into 6–8 portions, then take off the cling film. Place a spoonful of the purée on each plate and arrange a slice of the terrine on top. Mix the apple and shallot rings with a little olive oil and arrange around the terrine, along with a few micro leaves, if using. Serve, if you like, with a basket of freshly toasted pain de campagne.

Chef's notes

If you don't have a pressure cooker you can cook the meat on the stove. Put the ham hock and pig's trotter into a large stockpot or saucepan, cover with 2.5 litres of cold water and bring to the boil. Skim to remove the impurities. Allow to bubble gently for 1 minute. Turn down the heat to a gentle simmer, add the apple juice, celery, onion, bouquet garni and black peppercorns and put the lid on, leaving a slight gap. Cook for 3–4 hours, adding all the vegetables 45 minutes before the end of the cooking time, then continue with the recipe.

The excess cooking stock can be used as a wonderfully simple soup or as a broth to cook noodles.

The rind from the ham hock is not fat; it is collagen. It can be chopped into 1cm cubes and put back into the terrine mixure to add texture.

Variations

Pig's ears or snout, cooked at the same time as the ham hock, can be chopped up and added to the terrine to give it a different texture.

The terrine can be served with a range of accompaniments, such as pickled mushrooms or salad leaves.

You can make a simple parsley oil to mix with the apple and shallots instead of the olive oil. Line a fine sieve with muslin and place over a glass bowl. Put 150g of roughly chopped flat-leaf parsley, 250ml of olive oil and a pinch of sea salt into a blender and blend on full speed for 1 minute. Pour the parsley oil through the lined sieve and push with the back of a spoon to extract as much oil as possible. Taste and adjust the seasoning if required. Set aside in the fridge until needed.

APPLE CHARLOTTE

I'm still amazed at how a dish can be so strongly reminiscent of your childhood – a smell, a particular season and, of course, the feeling of that long wait for dessert. This is an elegant version of a very rustic Charlotte that my mum would make with leftover bread. It is a lighter version than the classic recipe – much lower in butter – and it has a wonderful texture and very clean, clear flavours. You will notice that I have used two varieties of apple – with very good reason. The Cox's Orange Pippin has acidity and is wonderfully firm, while the Blenheim Orange begs to be puréed. The combination is what creates the magic. *Bon appétit!*

SERVES 6–8

Preparation time: 15 minutes
Cooking time: 50 minutes

For the caramelised apples
80g caster sugar
25g unsalted butter, chilled
500g Cox's Orange Pippin apples, peeled, cored and each cut into 8 wedges

For the compote
150ml fresh apple juice
10g caster sugar
½ tsp apple pectin
250g Blenheim Orange apples (about 5), peeled and chopped
½ tsp Vanilla Purée (see page 281) or good-quality vanilla extract

For the cake ring
50g unsalted butter, softened
50g caster sugar

For the caramelised apples, in a large sauté pan on a medium–high heat, bring the sugar to a dark golden caramel stage, then add the butter. The caramel will emulsify with the butter and the cold butter will also stop the cooking of the caramel. Add the apples and cook in the caramel for 5 minutes, with a lid on, until they soften but still hold their shape; the centre will still be a little raw. Remove from the heat.

For the compote, mix 50ml of the apple juice with the sugar and pectin. Slide the chopped apple into a medium saucepan on a medium heat, add the remaining apple juice and cook for 10 minutes, covered with a lid, until the apples break down.

Add the sugar/pectin mix and vanilla purée or extract, stir and cook for a further 5 minutes to allow any moisture to evaporate. Remove from the heat.

Preheat the oven to 210°C/Gas Mark 6½.

To prepare the cake ring, lightly butter the inside of a 15 x 6cm cake ring. Dip the ring in sugar so that the sugar coats the inside of the ring. Tap it lightly to ensure an even coating; tap off any excess.

Lay out a 25 x 25cm piece of foil, then cover it with the same size of parchment paper. Place the cake ring on top and roll up the foil and paper, so the foil holds tightly to the bottom of the ring – this will prevent any juices escaping. Place the ring on a flat baking tray.

Continued overleaf →

For the Charlotte

200g wholemeal bread, cut into 11 slices; each 5mm thick

50g unsalted butter, softened

For the Charlotte, cut the slices of bread into 6 x 6cm squares. Lightly spread both sides of the bread with the butter and pan-fry in a large frying pan on a medium–high heat for 20–30 seconds on one side, until evenly golden brown. Transfer the bread to a plate or tray then use it to line the inside of the ring, browned sides facing outwards and overlapping by 2cm. Press to ensure they stick to the sides.

To build, mix the caramelised apple into the compote, then pour the mixture into the centre of the ring to fill the Charlotte. It will look too much and there will be a slight dome, but after cooking the apples will collapse under their own weight until they are level with the rim of the ring. Place the apple Charlotte in the oven for 30 minutes. Remove from the oven and leave to cool completely for a minimum of 3 hours. This will allow the pectin to set fully and firm up, which will also make the Charlotte easier to slice. Once cool, turn the Charlotte upside down by placing a large plate on top and flipping it over. Remove the foil and paper from the ring. You will need to heat the ring a little to lift it off smoothly; either use a blowtorch or place in an oven heated to 180°C/Gas Mark 4 for 1 minute, then ease it off gently.

To serve, carefully cut the Charlotte into 6–8 pieces. This beautiful dessert can be served with vanilla ice cream or Crème Chantilly (see page 156). It's also perfect with a glass of your best cider.

CHICORY

'IN THE BLANC FAMILY HOUSEHOLD the rhythm of the year completely defined what we ate, because most of it was grown in the garden,' says Raymond. 'Salad leaves were not only for summer. We grew different varieties for each of the four seasons: some peppery, some sweet, some bitter, with different textures and shapes – soft, crunchy, curly. 'For me, winter leaves are all about the bitter flavours and sculptural shapes of the chicory family.'

The chicory genus is a large and often confusing one, spanning many shapes and colours, from the pale-leaved Witloof to spiky green frisée and ruby red radicchio.

The members of this botanical genus, *Cichorium*, can cause confusion, largely because throughout the world they often go by interchangeable names. For example, the pale yellow and white egg-shaped head of crisp pointed leaves that in Britain we simply call chicory is known as endive in the USA and Belgian endive in France, alluding to the fact that this style of chicory hails originally from Belgium, where it is known as Witloof, or 'white leaf'. In Britain, however, we use the name curly endive to describe frizzy-leafed heads of frisée but in France this is known as *chicorée frisée*.

The simple way to look at it is that the genus encompasses Witloof chicory and all the other varieties grown for their hearts or loose leaves, including the light green sugar loaf and the red-leafed, white-veined varieties that we know by the Italian name of radicchio; as well as frisée, the curly broader-leaved escarole (also known as Batavian) and dandelion. 'As children we used to go out searching for dandelion leaves – wonderfully bitter', recalls Raymond. 'Wherever there were mole hills, you would find them. What prizes; we would bring baskets of them home, and my mother would use them in a salad, or flash-fry them with lardons.

When it comes to frisée, he says, 'I love the sturdier heads, with quite thick leaves and a full-on bitter flavour. In France you see enormous, glorious, perfectly-shaped ones. Don't talk to me about the fine, spindly variety, that I call "Parisien" frisée; it doesn't compare.'

'I had always thought of both frisée and chicory as bit of a mystery and a challenge – even though my parents produced them without a thought – because they both need the gardener's craft. In the case of frisée, you need to blanch the heart of it (see page 227) to give it that wonderful yellow tender centre – and Witloof chicory has to be finished in darkness in controlled temperatures to produce its pale leaves and delicate taste. But I was determined to crack the code! Even more so after I visited a local school as part of a project to get children cooking and growing, and the kids presented me with 12 pots of perfectly formed, blanched Belgian endive! To add insult to injury, they had even grown some red varieties as well. I said to Anna, 'We have to learn to do this, otherwise the children will put us to shame!'

Witloof chicory has its origins in a similar historical fluke to that which first produced forced rhubarb at the Chelsea Physic Garden (see page 38). In this case, a Brussels farmer Jan Lammers went away to join the revolution fighting for Belgian independence in 1830, leaving some chicory roots in the dark of his cellar. At the time, all over Europe and in many other countries through India, South East Asia, South Africa and America, chicory was grown primarily for its roots, which were baked, ground and then used as a substitute for, or addition to, coffee.

Lammers had been intending to use the roots in this way, but on his return from war he discovered that the roots had sprouted small, white, tender leaves in the darkness of the cellar, which tasted crunchy, slightly bitter and quite beautiful.

By the 1870s this new style of chicory had grown so much in popularity that in Paris it was known as 'white gold'.

Above: Radicchio on a frosty morning, and opposite: engraving of chicory, (Cichorium intybus) from Joseph Jacob Plenck's Icones Plantarum Medicinalium, *vol. 6: t.586 (1788–1812).*

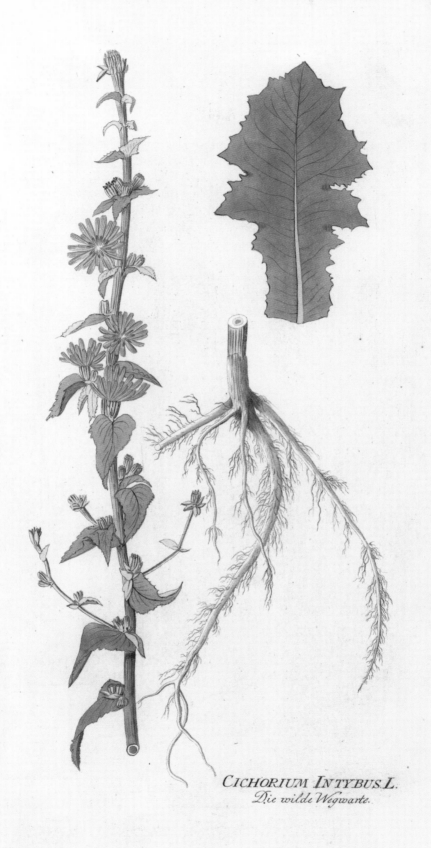

Cichorium Intybus. L.
Die wilde Wegwarte.

Left: The stunning hues of radicchio stand out in a bed of mixed winter lettuces, including frisée and escarole.

GROWING NOTES

WITLOOF CHICORY (BELGIAN ENDIVE)

Bear in mind this is a plant that is intended to be 'blanched' or 'forced', i.e. it is grown outside where it develops deep roots and green foliage, then lifted and brought inside in the winter and kept in the dark, subjected first to a period of cold and then warmth. The darkness stops the process of photosynthesis, and the change of temperature tricks the plant into thinking it has gone from winter into spring, so it will shoot out its tender, pale leaves. Done commercially, this forcing relies on specific temperature control, and although you can do it on a small scale at home, if you haven't tried it before, it is best to treat it as a bit of fun, and not bank on perfect results. If you want to try it, this is what to do:

Sow the seeds directly into the soil between May and early June (in this case don't add well-rotted manure or compost in advance, as Witloof prefers less fertile soil). Sow in shallow 7mm drills (furrows): one or two seeds every 12.5cm, and if sowing more than one row, leave a space of 50cm between each row. Once the seedlings are established, thin out every other one, to leave 25cm between each remaining plant, as they need plenty of room to form a decent-sized root (the energy-store needed for the forcing process).

To start the forcing process, in November dig up the plants and transfer them to large containers filled with spent compost or sand. Trim the tops of each plant back to 3.5cm above the top of the root and then cover the containers with buckets or dustbins to keep out the light.

First the containers need to be kept (still covered to exclude the light) in a cold place, such as a shed or a garage, for two weeks. In an ideal world the temperature would be 2–3°C but it shouldn't be higher than 5–6°C. If the temperature is at the upper end of the scale, it is best to leave the plants in this cold phase for up to three weeks.

Next, move the containers (still covered) into a warm room in the house or an airing cupboard, that is between 19–21°C, for three weeks. Again, you would ideally start off at 21°C for the first week, then lower the heat to 20°C in the second week and 19°C for the third week.

After this period of 5–6 weeks, you will hopefully have achieved some pale yellow-white heads of chicory that can be harvested with a sharp knife.

FRISÉE (CURLY ENDIVE)

Sow seeds (as for chicory) in mid-May through to mid-August for harvesting in the autumn.

About 12 weeks after sowing, when the heads are mature and quite open and sprawling, the hearts need to be 'blanched' in order to achieve a light yellow colour and temper the bitterness. The traditional way to do this is to tie a piece of string (or use an elastic band) around the whole head of the frisée so that it closes right up and blocks the light from the heart (make sure you do this when the leaves are absolutely dry, otherwise the heart can rot).

After about ten days of blanching the frisée will be ready to harvest by cutting the whole head with a sharp knife.

RAYMOND'S FLAVOUR NOTES

As well as being one of the key flavours that we respond to, along with sweet, sour, salty and umami – the bitterness that characterises the chicory family is important. Bitter compounds in chicory may be good for the health of the liver and are reputed to stimulate digestive juices.

Witloof chicory, which in France we know as Belgian endive, knows its season and it loves being put with walnuts, apples, Conference pears, Roquefort and blue cheeses. It is also lovely blanched briefly in boiling water, then pan-fried so that it caramelises. And of course,

one of the great easy Belgian family recipes is a gratin of endives, each one blanched, then wrapped in a slice of ham and baked in cheese sauce (see my recipe on page 228).

The red-leafed radicchio is wonderfully bitter in the salad bowl, along with frisée and escarole, but like chicory, radicchio is also good quickly pan-fried, so that it is still almost raw, but so that some of its sugars come out and its edges just start to brown and caramelise.

Left: Cichorium intybus *from* English Botany, Or, Coloured Figures of British Plants, *vol. 8: t. 539 (1799) by James Edward Smith, founder of the Linnean Society, the world's oldest natural history society. Illustration by James Sowerby.*

CHICORY GRATIN

A beloved classic of Belgian cooking; this is a simple, rustic family dish. The ham used would normally be Paris ham but York ham or your local smoked ham would be fantastic. The Comté cheese, which is from my home region, can be replaced by any British cheese. And, of course, omit the ham for a vegetarian version.

SERVES 2

Preparation time: 5 minutes
Cooking time: 1 hour

For the chicory
4 heads yellow chicory
1 tbsp lemon juice
1 tbsp sugar
2 large pinches sea salt
6 white peppercorns
600ml water

For the chard
100ml water
10g unsalted butter
2 small Swiss chard stalks with leaves, chop the stalks into 1cm pieces; roughly chop the leaves

For the cheese sauce
35g unsalted butter
35g plain flour
450ml whole milk
100g Comté cheese, finely grated
1 tbsp Dijon mustard
pinch sea salt
pinch freshly ground white pepper

To assemble the gratin
4 slices cooked ham
50g Comté cheese, finely grated

To cook the chicory, place in a medium saucepan with the lemon juice, sugar, salt and peppercorns and add enough of the water to barely cover. Place on a medium heat, cover with a cartouche and a lid smaller than the diameter of the pan (this is to keep the chicory submerged) and bring to the boil. Reduce the heat and simmer for 45–60 minutes. It is important to cook the chicory slowly to remove most of its bitterness. Turn off the heat, lift the chicory on to a wire rack to cool and allow the moisture to escape. Once cool, gently press out any extra moisture with a tea towel.

Preheat the oven to 190°C/Gas Mark 5.

To cook the chard stalks, put the water and butter into a medium saucepan on a high heat. Cook the chard stalks for 20 minutes, adding more water if necessary. Once tender, lift out the stalks and cook the leaves for 3 minutes. Strain, mix the stalks and leaves and arrange in a small gratin dish.

While the chard is cooking, make the cheese sauce. In a small saucepan on a medium heat, melt the butter. Add the flour, whisk until smooth and cook to a nutty blond colour. Take the pan off the heat, whisk in the milk and return to a medium heat. Cook for a further 4 minutes, stirring constantly with the whisk until the sauce thickens. It is important to cook it for at least 4 minutes as the starch needs this time to swell, which thickens the sauce. Add the cheese and mustard and cook for 3 minutes, stirring, until the cheese has fully melted. Remove from the heat, taste and adjust the seasoning if required.

To assemble the gratin, fold the ham slices in half and arrange one chicory head on each slice. Pack tightly in the gratin dish, then spoon over the cheese sauce, sprinkle with the Comté cheese. Bake in the top part of the oven for 25 minutes. The top is the hottest part of the oven and the air circulation will help ensure your gratin gains its wonderful golden brown colour.

CHICORY TART WITH ORANGE DRESSING

In the UK, chicory is often confined to the salad bowl, which is such a shame as cooking can enhance its unique flavour profile. Here I have slow-cooked and pan-fried chicory so that it caramelises. The contrast between the bitterness of the leaves and their sweet caramel-tinged edges is fantastic. I've also added a little extra acidity and sweetness to the dish with an orange dressing. Using tapioca in a dressing might sound a little strange addition, and it is optional, but it adds an interesting texture and I'd urge you to give it a try.

SERVES 4, AS A STARTER

Preparation time: 15 minutes, plus chilling
Cooking time: 1 hour

For the pickled shallots

1.1 litres water
2 tsp sea salt
12 grey griselle shallots, peeled
60ml red wine vinegar
40g caster sugar
pinch sea salt
pinch freshly ground black pepper
½ star anise
1 small thyme sprig

For the chicory

2 heads yellow chicory
1 tsp lemon juice
300ml water
1 tsp sugar
ground white pepper
20g unsalted butter
sea salt and freshly ground white pepper

For the pickled shallots, in a medium saucepan on a high heat bring 1 litre of the water and the salt to the boil and blanch the shallots for 2 minutes. Drain, then return the shallots to the saucepan with the remaining 100ml of water, the vinegar, sugar, salt, pepper, star anise and thyme. Bring to the boil and simmer for 2–3 minutes, until they are tender but retain a little bit of texture. Remove from the heat and allow to cool in the cooking liquor before storing in a sealed container in the fridge.

To cook the chicory, in a small saucepan on a medium heat, mix all the ingredients apart from the butter with a large pinch of salt and a pinch of pepper. Cover with a lid and bring to the boil. Reduce the heat and simmer for 50 minutes. It is important to cook the chicory slowly to soften the texture and to allow time for the carbohydrates in the chicory to transform the bitterness into sweetness. Turn off the heat, lift the chicory on to a wire rack to cool and allow the moisture to escape. Once cool, using a tea towel, gently press out any extra moisture. Slice each chicory in half lengthways.

In a medium frying pan on a medium heat, gently pan-fry and colour the chicory, cut-side down, in the butter for 6–8 minutes. Season with a pinch of salt and pepper. Remove, place on a tray and reserve.

Preheat the oven to 180°C/Gas Mark 4.

Continued overleaf $\rightarrow$

For building and cooking the tart

200g puff pastry,

1 egg yolk, beaten

1 batch Onion Jam (see page 198)

10g unsalted butter, melted

For the orange dressing

100ml fresh orange juice

30g liquid glucose

2 tsp Chardonnay vinegar

1½ tbsp extra virgin olive oil

pinch cayenne pepper

pinch orange zest powder
  (optional; orange zest dried in
  the oven at 100°C/Gas Mark ¼
  for 1 hour, then blitzed to a
  powder)

30g tapioca, boiled for 10 minutes,
  until tender, then rinsed under
  cold water (optional)

To serve

micro leaves (optional)

To build the tart, on a lightly floured surface, roll out the pastry until 3mm thick, Refrigerate for 15 minutes to firm up the dough. When cold, cut out four 12 x 7cm rectangles. Lay the four rectangles of rolled pastry on a non-stick baking tray. Brush the top lightly with egg yolk, then spread a quarter of the onion jam down the centre of each rectangle. Top with one half of caramelised chicory, cut-side up, and press down lightly to secure it, then brush the top of the chicory with melted butter. Bake in the oven for 15 minutes, until the pastry is golden brown. Remove and transfer to a wire rack to cool slightly before serving.

For the dressing, in a small saucepan on a high heat, bring the orange juice, glucose, vinegar, olive oil and cayenne pepper to a boil for 3 minutes, until it has reduced by half. Remove from the heat, add the orange zest powder and leave to cool. Once cool, mix in a small bowl with the cooked tapioca, taste and adjust the seasoning if required.

To serve, place the warm chicory tart in the centre of each plate, spoon the orange dressing around and arrange pickled shallots and microleaves, if using, either side.

TURNIPS

'**THERE** IS ONLY ONE TURNIP FOR ME, the Demi-long de Croissy, the best flavoured I have found. So much of the way we feel about food connects with family, and I have an emotional attachment to it because it was first planted in the garden of my restaurant by my father,' says Raymond. 'When I first arrived and saw that garden, there was only about one acre given over to vegetables, but it was a tangle of weeds, with rabbits everywhere. I thought, "*mon Dieu*, what am I going to do?" But I had a plan: payback time for my father for all those childhood years of digging and planting and harvesting that I had done in our garden at home, with my father presiding over us kids like a field martial! So my papa came to Oxfordshire and spent three months (as my commis!) preparing the ground for me and digging in compost, and he brought with him his favourite seeds, including the Demi-long de Croissy. It grows quite large and long – it's like a parsnip with very fine skin – so it is very economical. It is a turnip that isn't at all woody or grainy and it has so much character; not bitter, but slightly sweet and nutty. The Demi-long de Croissy is an iconic heritage vegetable for me – beautiful, but also a symbol of sweet revenge!'

In Britain, turnip is often confused with swede, despite the fact that they are botanically separate.

Oddly, given that there is little obvious resemblance between a smooth, hard turnip and a cabbage or head of kale, turnips are part of the brassica group of 'cruciferous' vegetables, as they are often known, because they all bear flowers which have four petals in the shape of a cross (for more on brassicas turn to pages 257–70).

The Romans, who introduced so many of our familiar garden vegetables to Britain, appear to have given us turnips, though the vegetable has rarely inspired the respect or popularity it evokes in other countries. Instead, the preference in Britain tends to be for swede, which despite being in the same species as turnip, is botanically separate and has a different history. Furthermore, the two are often confused. It doesn't help that in Cornwall, locals have always referred to swede as turnip, so when purists insist that turnip is an essential ingredient in the traditional Cornish pasty, they actually mean swede! Likewise, in Scotland 'bashed neeps' really refers to swedes (coarsely mashed with butter and served with haggis) – and not turnips as the name suggests.

In seventeenth-century Britain, turnips were grown primarily for animal fodder, and as such had a part to play in the revolution in farming practices that took place at this time, when Viscount Charles 'Turnip' Townshend was credited with introducing a new four-year crop rotation system, involving clover and turnips. Peasant farming had used a system of crop rotation since medieval times, but the practice had been to operate a

Turnips had an important part to play in the development of crop rotation in seventeenth-century British agriculture.

three-year cycle, and then leave one field fallow each year. Townshend, together with Jethro Tull, the inventor of the seed drill, introduced turnips as a fourth-year crop. As well as providing feed for the cattle and so increasing meat production, the turnips, along with clover, helped to restore the fertility of the land by adding nitrates back into the soil.

Other cultures have traditionally given the turnip a much more important place in the kitchen. 'My mother always put turnip into a winter soup,' says Raymond. 'We had a soup for every season, and in winter it would be a balance of turnip, for some pepperiness; onions and potatoes, which are neutral and would thicken the soup, and carrot, for sweetness; plus whatever herbs there were in the garden. Everything would go into the *cocotte minute* (pressure cooker), then the soup would be puréed and brought to the table. It was such a fantastic, fast and easy way to cook and keep all the nutrients in the vegetables – especially if you had a big, busy family of seven, like ours. Or she would put turnips into a humble *pot-au-feu*. Pork or chicken would be covered with water, brought to the boil, skimmed, and then the vegetables would go in: big chunks of turnip, carrots and onions, then it would be brought to the boil again and simmered very slowly until everything was cooked.'

Opposite: An illustration of a turnip, Brassica rapa, *loose print from an unidentified publication, Kew Illustrations Collections.*

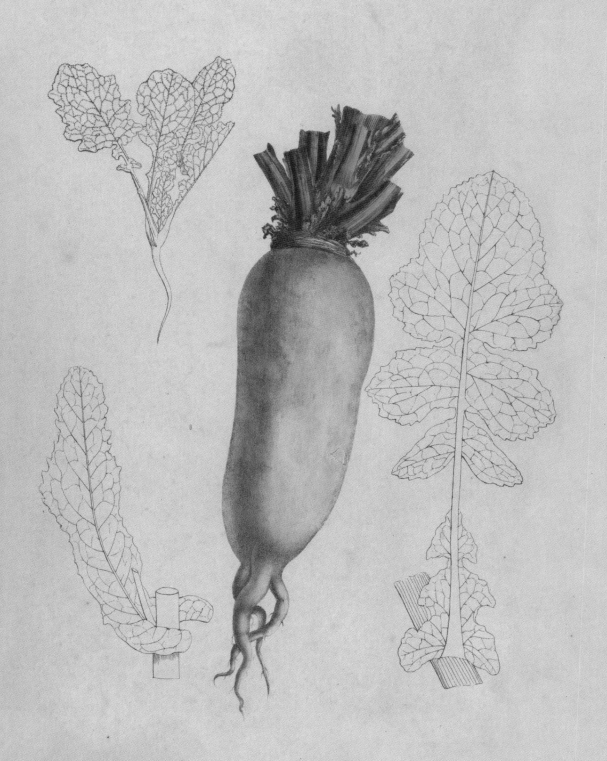

Left: Turnips, netted against pigeons and the Kew peacocks, take pride of place beyond a bed of 'companion' planted golden tagetes (French marigolds). In the background, other members of the brassica group lend definition to the garden with their statuesque shapes.

GROWING NOTES

The turnips planted at Kew showcase varieties which, if planted in succession, will see you through to winter. These include Raymond's favourite heritage Demi-long de Croissy and Purple Top Milan, an heirloom Italian variety which is fast-growing, small and sweet. These can be sown every few weeks from March to August, and will be ready to pull up from May to October. Other heritage varieties such as Golden Ball make a good winter crop when sown in mid- to late summer for harvesting from October through to November/December.

Dig in some well-rotted compost or manure in the autumn before planting.

Sow the seeds thinly in drills (furrows) around 1–2cm deep. The seedlings will come up very quickly and as soon as they are about 10cm tall, thin them to around 10–15cm apart for smaller early varieties, and 25cm for larger maincrop ones. If growing more than one row, leave 30cm between each row.

'Like other brassicas, such as cabbages and kale, turnips can be a magnet for pigeons,' says Alice. 'And at Kew we also have peacocks who love them! So cover your crops with fleece early on as a precaution. If pigeons persist once you take off the fleece (you need to do this when the plants are starting to push against it), you might have to cover the plants with nets.'

Keep the plants well weeded and water them in dry spells.

Seedlings can also be damaged by flea beetle, which might be black, metallic green or blue with a yellow stripe. The larvae will eat the

Above: Raymond's favourite Demi-long de Croissy turnip holds memories of his father.

roots, while the adults go for the leaves, making small holes in them and turning them brown. Horticultural fleece covering the plants (pegged down at the the corners) can help. Once the plants have grown enough to push against the fleece you can remove it, as the plants should now be robust enough to grow through any attack.

Clubroot is a soil-borne disease specific to the brassica family, that might sometimes affect turnips (see page 262 for more on this).

Unlike swedes, turnips do not store, so eat them as you pull them up. Or pickle them to preserve them (see recipe on page 242).

RAYMOND'S FLAVOUR NOTES

For an early turnip, my favourite will always be the heritage Demi-long de Croissy. Later on Golden Ball is another good heritage variety.

I know people can dislike the flavour of turnip, most likely because they have eaten it stewed for a long time. I think the way to convert people is to make a turnip and potato gratin. The turnip gives a lovely richness to the potato, and it has more length of flavour.

Alternatively cut them into small pieces and cook them quickly in an emulsion of butter and water (see page 17).

You can eat turnip raw, finely grated, like beetroot.

Something that is lovely to do is to slice turnips very finely on a mandoline, and do the same with some carrots and fennel, then put them into a bowl of iced water. They will swell up a little and curl and their powerful flavours will soften a little. When you lift them from the bowl and dry them they are beautiful and crunchy, perfect for dipping into a rich mayonnaise or yoghurt.

And you can also dry them into crisps in the oven. Slice them very finely and lay them on baking parchment on a baking tray, then put them into the oven at 100°C/Gas Mark ¼ for 1 hour, until crunchy.

Left and above: Veitch's Red Globe is a heritage variety that dates back to 1838.

CURED SPICED TURNIP AND SWEDE; SHORT RIBS

Curing the turnip and swede in a salt and spice mixture creates a few small miracles. It extracts the water, which changes both the texture and the flavour and ensures the vegetables aren't watery; secondly it creates an extraordinary canvas of sour, sweet, acidity and spice. Curing also has the advantage of semi-preserving the vegetables so they can be prepared up to two weeks in advance and kept in the fridge.

SERVES 4

Preparation time: 4 hours
Cooking time: 4 hours

For the spiced turnip and swede
450g turnips, peeled and thinly
    sliced
200g swede, peeled and thinly
    sliced
6 juniper berries, ground to a
    powder
2 cloves, ground to a powder
grating of mace
1 heaped tsp sea salt
pinch caster sugar
pinch cayenne pepper
3 tbsp duck fat
1½ tbsp Chardonnay vinegar
1 tbsp gin

For the beef ribs (optional)
large pinch five-spice powder
1 tsp sea salt
1 tsp freshly ground black pepper
2.5g garlic granules
1 tbsp rapeseed oil
1.2kg beef ribs (4 bones)

For the basting sauce
150ml hoisin sauce
55ml sake, rice wine or dry sherry
30ml acacia honey
2 garlic cloves, puréed
10g root ginger, peeled and grated

For the spiced turnip and swede, in a large bowl, mix the turnip and swede with the juniper berries, cloves, mace, salt, sugar and cayenne pepper. Set aside for 3 hours for the vegetable juices to release and exchange flavours.

In a large sauté pan on a high heat, sweeten the turnip and swede in the duck fat. Lower to a medium heat and sweat for 5 minutes, stirring occasionally. The vegetables should be slightly soft but still have a little bite to provide some texture. Stir in the vinegar and gin, taste and adjust the seasoning if required. The spiced vegetables can be stored in an airtight container in the fridge for up to two weeks

To marinate the beef ribs, in a small bowl mix the five spice, salt, pepper, garlic granules and oil, then massage into the beef. Leave at room temperature for 4 hours, or overnight if you can.

The next day, preheat the oven to 160°C/Gas Mark 3. Sit the beef ribs in a small roasting tin and roast for 1 hour.

For the basting sauce, mix all the ingredients in a bowl.

Remove the ribs from the oven to a large piece of foil. Baste with half the basting sauce and wrap tightly in the foil. Return to the oven for another 2 hours. The beef will steam in its own juices.

Unwrap the beef and place back in the roasting tin; pour its juices into the remaining basting sauce. Give the beef a final basting with the sauce then return to the oven for an hour. Baste the beef every 15 minutes to create layers of caramelised crust.

At this stage the meat should be melting and falling away from the bone. Should you have any basting sauce left then give the beef a final brush and serve with the spiced turnip and swede.

GRILLED MACKEREL, PICKLED TURNIPS AND APPLE

Pickled turnips are popular in Japanese cuisine, but my mother would also pickle the turnips we grew at home to preserve them. Here, the turnip's characteristic bitter flavour has been mellowed by the mixture of acidity and sweetness in the pickling liquor and it provides a perfect foil for the richness of the oily fish.

SERVES 4

Marinating time: 6–12 hours
Cooking time: 5 minutes

For marinating the mackerel

1 coriander sprig (with root if
    possible), chopped
grated zest of ¼ lime, plus a
    squeeze of juice to finish
10g root ginger, peeled and grated
pinch coriander seeds, lightly
    toasted and finely ground
¼ garlic clove, puréed
pinch sea salt
4 tsp extra virgin olive oil
4 mackerel fillets (about 100g each)

For the apple and ginger purée

2 Cox's Orange Pippin apples,
    peeled, cored and diced
3g root ginger, peeled and grated
dash of lemon juice
pinch caster sugar (optional)

For the pickled turnip

pared zest and juice of 1 lime
4 tbsp sake
1 tbsp mirin
1 tbsp rice wine vinegar
100ml water
large pinch sea salt
2 tsp palm sugar
2g root ginger, finely sliced
140g turnip, sliced into 2mm discs
    on a mandolin

To marinate the mackerel, in a small bowl, mix together the fresh coriander, lime zest, ginger, coriander seeds, garlic, salt and olive oil. Score the mackerel fillets at 1cm intervals so the spices can penetrate. Put the mackerel fillets on to a small tray, skin-side down, and, using a pastry brush, spread the marinade over each fillet. Cover with cling film and place in the fridge for a minimum of 6 hours and up to 12 hours. The spiced oil will cut through some of the richness of the mackerel and also sharpen the flavour.

For the apple and ginger purée, put the apples, ginger and 2 tablespoons of water into a small casserole and simmer for 10 minutes until the apple has cooked down. Puree the apple using a hand-blender, adding some lemon juice to obtain the perfect consistency. Taste, add a pinch of sugar or dash more lemon juice if necessary and keep in the fridge.

For the pickled turnip, in a large saucepan on a high, heat bring all the ingredients except the turnips to the boil and boil for 1 minute. Add the turnip and cook for a further minute. Take off the heat, taste and check the turnip's flavour and texture, adding more seasoning if necessary. Cool at room temperature for 30 minutes, then cover and refrigerate. The pickle can be stored for up to a week.

Continued overleaf $\rightarrow$

For the glaze

juice of 1 lime

1 tbsp Manuka honey

2 tbsp light soy sauce

½ tsp finely grated peeled root
   ginger

To serve

micro leaves

For the glaze, in a small saucepan on a medium heat, bring three quarters of the lime juice and all the other ingredients to a gentle boil for 1 minute, to reduce it to a glaze. Remove from the heat and stir in the remaining lime juice. Set aside.

To cook the mackerel, remove the fillets from the fridge 30 minutes before cooking. Preheat the grill to its highest setting. Brush the glaze on to the skin and leave for 10 minutes for the glaze to dry. Glaze a second time. Place the mackerel fillets, skin-side up, on a lightly-oiled tray and grill for 4–5 minutes according to their size. They will crisp and gain an appetising dark amber colour. Finish with a squeeze of lime juice and a pinch of salt.

To serve, drain the turnip discs and arrange on each plate. Spread a spoonful of the purée alongside. Arrange the grilled mackerel across the turnip and purée and drizzle some of the cooking juices around the dish.

LEEKS

ALONG

WITH THE DRAGON AND THE DAFFODIL the leek is emblematic of Wales, yet exactly why is lost in myth and legend. Some say that in 640AD King Cadwaladr of Gwynedd and his men, in a victorious battle against invading Saxons, wore leeks in their helmets in order to identify each other. Others say the battle itself took place in a field of leeks.

Myth and legend surround the leek as an emblem of Wales, but whatever the truth, it was the Romans who introduced the garden variety to Britain.

In other stories it was in a different battle that Saint David told the soldiers to wear leeks in their caps; while the English poet Michael Drayton, in his epic poem on England and Wales, 'Poly-Olbion', published in 1612, wrote that during a time of contemplation and fasting Saint David:

'... fed upon the Leeks he gather'd in the fields.
In memory of whom, in the revolving year,
The Welch-men on his day that sacred herb do wear.'

In Shakespeare's *Henry V* the Welsh army captain Fluellen, surrounded by the dead on the battlefield after an improbable British victory at Agincourt, reinforces the legend when he says to the king, 'If your majesties is remembered of it, the Welshmen did good service in a garden where leeks did grow, wearing leeks in their Monmouth caps... and I do believe your majesty takes no scorn to wear the leek upon Saint Davy's day.' To which the King replies: 'I wear it for a memorable honour; For I am Welsh, you know, good countryman.'

Some historians believe that the emblem of the leek for the Welsh dates back to the time of the druids on the Island of Anglesey, who valued the vegetable for its medicinal properties. Whatever the truth, it is thought that while wild leeks most likely grew in Britain's forests, it was the Romans who first introduced the cultivated garden leek. The Romans certainly valued them in cooking. Recipes in *Apicius De Re Coquinaria* (see page 68) include leeks baked with cumin and pepper, broth and condensed wine must. And Pliny the Elder, the Roman writer, recorded in his *Natural History* that the leek had achieved celebrity status, since the Emperor Nero apparently ate 'leeks and oil every month, upon stated days, abstaining from every other kind of food,' as he believed they improved his voice.

The first sighting of leeks in Britain for Raymond, however, evokes quite different emotions. 'I always remember the big scary gardener at the restaurant where I began my cooking career,' he says. 'He grew leeks the size of tree trunks, and I was astonished to find that there were competitions held all over the country to see who could grow the biggest. I love to see leeks growing in the garden in winter, when only they and the brassicas are standing proud from the black, barren earth. They look so beautiful, standing to attention in their rows, like little soldiers with their green "flags" waving – but please, in the kitchen, don't use tree trunks!' The older and bigger a leek grows, the tougher it gets and the more strongly oniony it becomes in flavour.'

GROWING NOTES

Leeks don't like compacted soil, so in the autumn before planting dig some well-rotted manure or compost into the beds.

'The traditional thing to do is to create a seed bed in a different area of the garden in well-prepared soil in March or April,' says Joe. 'Just make a drill (furrow) about 1–1.5cm deep and sow the seeds thinly.'

'In the second half of May,' says Joe, 'when the young plants are pencil-thick and have developed a good root system, they can be lifted and moved to their permanent home in the prepared beds.'

Some people say that you need to trim the roots and tops of the plants before planting, but this isn't necessary. Make a hole for each leek that is at least 15cm deep, using a dibber. This depth is needed as the part of the stem that is beneath the soil and sees no light will be 'blanched' white. Since the white of the leek is the part that is mainly used for cooking, you want this to grow as long as possible.

Space the young leeks 22–30cm apart, and if you are planting more than one row, leave 30–38cm between each row. Keeping the leeks well spaced increases the airflow around the plants, which helps to prevent diseases like rust.

Instead of filling in the holes with soil, fill them with water. This is known as 'puddling in' – it settles the soil around the roots.

Keep well weeded and water in dry conditions until the leeks are well established.

Like garlic and onions, leeks are susceptible to onion white rot and leek rust (see page 117 for more information on these).

Leek moth caterpillars and the larvae of Allium leaf miner can also be a problem. They tunnel into the leaves, causing white patches. In some cases the plants will rot and die. Protect against the females moths and flies laying eggs by surrounding the plants with horticultural fleece.

From autumn onwards you can lift the leeks carefully using a garden fork, as soon as you feel they are big enough to use. Depending on the variety, you can harvest through the winter and sometimes on into April.

RAYMOND'S FLAVOUR NOTES

Of those we grew, my favourites were Jaune de Poitou and Bleu de Solaise, both French heritage varieties.

As with many vegetables, there is a flavour arc in the life of a leek. Very small young ones have a designer element that chefs love, but for me the flavour isn't formed enough. A medium-sized leek is perfect, before it grows big and fibrous and tastes powerfully oniony.

When you prepare a leek, use just the white part, and remove the first two outer shiny, hard layers, which are the most harsh and fibrous, then you will get to the matt layers, which tell you that you have reached the tender heart. Never waste anything: chop up these outer layers, and the green parts of the leek, and add them to soup.

In France there is a saying that leek is the asparagus of the poor, but for me the leek makes some wonderful dishes that you long to eat, and the greatest is leeks vinaigrette, a favourite family dish. You have to 'overcook' the leeks, simmering just the white parts until they are very tender. Serve them tepid, dressed with a classic mustard dressing, or a vinaigrette and some hard-boiled egg on top if you want to be festive. Wonderful.

Then there is vichyssoise, the great leek and potato soup, which marries the gentle starchiness of the potato with the stronger, yet refined oniony-garlicky flavour of the leek.

And gratin: leeks nestled in a cheese sauce made with a little mustard, with some Comté cheese grated on top and served with some ham, makes a great comforting winter dish.

Leeks also have an affinity with earthy winter black truffles and morel mushrooms. I have fond memories of one of the first dishes I created, a terrine of green and yellow leeks and langoustines, studded with black truffle. You'll find a simpler version on page 254.

Left: Alice sows using a stretch of string as a guide when planting into a drill (or shallow furrow) in a traditional seed bed.

LEEK AND SHELLFISH CHOWDER

Although the term 'chowder' is used across the world and you might think there is a 'classic' recipe, in fact the dish has no specific place of birth or defining ingredients and each country has its own interpretation. Mine is a simple light vegetable and shellfish soup. If you want to give it more richness and a little bulk, add some crisp grilled or pan-fried bacon or even smoked fish, or see the variations below. Make sure you choose fresh mussels, which will be shiny, closed, heavy with seawater and have no 'fishy' smell.

SERVES 4

Preparation time: 20 minutes
Cooking time: 10 minutes

For the leeks and shellfish
200g clams, washed
200g mussels, washed, beards
    removed
200g cockles, washed
200ml white wine
30g unsalted butter
1 large leek, outer 5 layers
    removed and thinly sliced
1 onion, finely diced
1 garlic clove, sliced
1 bay leaf
300ml water
100ml whipping cream
2g root ginger, finely grated
    (optional)
 2 gratings of nutmeg, ground
    (optional)

To finish
20g unsalted butter
1 leek, cut into 3cm batons
100g (1 large) Red Duke of York
    potato, peeled and cut into
    1cm dice
lemon juice, to taste
10g wakame seaweed, rinsed
sea salt and freshly ground black
    pepper

To prepare the leeks and shellfish, ensure all the clams, mussels and cockles are tightly closed; any that are not should be discarded as they are dead. Put a large saucepan on to a high heat. Once hot, add the white wine and bring to the boil. Add the shellfish, cover with a lid and cook for 2–3 minutes, until all have opened (discard any that haven't). Pour into a bowl and cool slightly before picking out the flesh and discarding the shells. Set the flesh aside, strain the cooking liquor and reserve.

In a separate large saucepan on a medium heat, melt the butter and sweat the leek, onion, garlic and bay leaf for 5 minutes, until soft but with no colour. Add the reserved shellfish cooking liquor, water and cream. Bring to the boil, then add the ginger and nutmeg, if using, and simmer for 2 minutes.

To finish the chowder, in a small sauté pan on a medium heat, melt the butter and sweat the leek and potatoes for 5 minutes with a pinch of salt and pepper. Add 2 tablespoons of water and simmer for a further 3 minutes, until the potato is cooked through. Add the cooked shellfish and remove this soup garnish from the heat. Leave to one side whilst you blend the soup in a blender on full speed for 1 minute. Taste and adjust the seasoning with salt, pepper and lemon juice.

To serve, divide the hot soup between four bowls. Top with the garnish then scatter over the seaweed. Serve immediately

Variation
For an Indian version, add some Madras curry powder to the onion and then finish the dish with some lemon and coriander. For a Thai version, some chilli, garlic, lemongrass and lime leaf could be added to the onion and the cream replaced with coconut cream. To create a New England-style chowder, add 100g of chopped bacon to the onions at the beginning.

PRESSED LEEK TERRINE

Here I have taken one of my favourite classics from the French repertoire – leeks vinaigrette – and compressed it into a beautiful, flavoursome vegetarian terrine. The main recipe here gives you the option to layer leeks with some earthy black truffles, which are, of course, very extravagant and expensive, but they really are wonderful as a treat for a special occasion or celebration. For a humbler, rustic yet still very seasonal alternative, I've also shown you how to make the terrine with Jerusalem artichokes, whose gentle nutty flavour is a natural partner to the sweet leeks.

SERVES 6
Preparation time: 15 minutes
Cooking time: 25 minutes, plus
　　pressing
You will also need: 2 x plastic
　　containers measuring 15 x
　　16 x 5.5cm

For the leeks
12 leeks, trimmed to 15cm lengths
3 litres water
3 tsp sea salt

For the vinaigrette
4 tbsp hazelnut oil
1 tbsp Chardonnay wine vinegar,
1 tsp water
pinch sea salt
pinch freshly ground black pepper

To build the terrine
20g black truffle, very finely sliced
　　with a mandoline (optional)

For the terrine, double up a 30 x 30cm piece of cling film and use it to line one of the plastic containers so there is an overhang all around to wrap the terrine later.

Prepare the leeks by peeling off the two outer layers as they will be too fibrous. Divide each leek into two 15cm lengths; the trimmings can be used to make soup.

In a large saucepan on a high heat, bring the water and salt to a rolling boil. Cook the leeks for 20 minutes, until completely tender. Using a slotted spoon, lift on to a tray and let the steam escape. Leave to cool completely.

For the vinaigrette, in a medium bowl, whisk all the ingredients with a hand-held blender, taste and adjust the seasoning if necessary.

To build the terrine, layer the leeks tightly side by side in the lined container (8 pieces per layer) and brush with a little of the vinaigrette. Cover with a few of the truffle slices, if using, press down, then repeat for the second layer, alternating the white and greener parts of the leek. Continue until you have three layers of leek, then fold over the overhanging cling film, place the second plastic container on top and fill it with 1kg of weight to compress the terrine (you could use some tins of beans, for example). Leave for 12 hours or overnight. Store the vinaigrette in the fridge for serving.

Continued overleaf →

To serve

10 sprigs chopped chives

180g Jerusalem artichokes, peeled,
cut in half and steamed
for 10–15 minutes, until tender
or Pickled shallots (see page
231)

8g black truffle, very finely sliced
with a mandoline (optional)

small selection of winter leaves,
such as lamb's lettuce

.

To serve, lift the terrine from its container on to a chopping board, keeping the cling film wrapped around, which will keep the structure of the terrine when you slice it. Using a carving knife, slice the terrine into eight even slices, approximately 2cm thick. Carefully peel off the cling film and use a palette knife to transfer a slice to the centre of each plate. Whisk the chopped chives into the reserved vinaigrette, then brush it over the top of each slice of terrine. If serving with the Jerusalem artichokes, dress them with the remaining vinaigrette and scatter them around the terrine; alternatively scatter around the pickled shallots. Finish with some fine shavings of fresh truffle, if using, and winter leaves.

Cook's note

If you use truffles, slice them at the last minute and cover with cling film, otherwise their essential oils will disappear

Only stir the chopped chives into the vinaigrette just before you serve otherwise the strong onion scent will compete with the delicate flavours of the leeks.

Variation

For a cheaper and wonderfully seasonal and flavoursome alternative, pair the leeks with their friend the Jerusalem artichoke instead. Peel and halve 3 Jerusalem artichokes. Steam for 10–15 minutes, then season with salt and pepper. Cook and prepare the leeks as above, and before you lay the first layer of leeks in the container place a line of the artichokes down the centre of the terrine then continue as above, layering the leeks around the artichokes.

CABBAGE, BROCCOLI AND OTHER BRASSICAS

'I LOVE TO SEE BRASSICAS in the winter landscape, when much of the earth is bare and black, maybe dusted with frost or snow or shrouded with mist,' says Raymond. 'You think nothing could grow there, yet these enormous, awe-inspiring, sculptural, green and burgundy red cabbages, cavolo nero, broccoli and Brussels sprouts are rising up defiantly. When I look at them I see art.'

With their bold, sculptural shapes standing out in the winter landscape, brassicas bring drama to the garden.

For scientists as well as gardeners, the extensive brassica group affords an important, deep vein of interest and exploration. At Kew's Millenium Seed Bank in Wakehurst, some two billion seeds have been stored as part of the worldwide conservation programme. These seeds include those of Crop Wild Relatives, which have been collected as part of a project that focuses on preserving the seeds of the wild plants that are relatives of today's crops (many of which would otherwise face extinction). The programme studies the wild plants' characteristics and natural habitats in order to identify useful traits and use this in breeding to produce new varieties that will provide food security for future generations in ever-challenging climatic conditions.

Cabbage, kale, broccoli, Brussels sprouts and cauliflower (also known as cruciferous vegetables, see page 234), are all descended from the wild cabbage. However, over centuries of selective breeding and most recently, intensive, large-scale farming, 75 per cent of the genetic diversity of the original wild varieties has been lost. As Dr Ruth Eastwood, co-ordinator of the project, explains, since all the members of the related brassica crops are vulnerable to the same pests and diseases, there is a potential for a virulent attack to wipe them all out.

Brassicas have also been in the limelight in recent years for nutritional reasons. First broccoli, especially the fashionable purple sprouting variety, fêted as a superfood thanks to its vitamins, minerals and substances such as sulforaphane that may help to reduce the risk of cancer. And now kale is on every smart menu, hailed as a powerhouse of antioxidants, anti-inflammatories and provitamins A and K.

'The kale family is one I was quite late in discovering,' says Raymond, 'as I never tasted it when I was growing up. But I love it. It is so full of iron-intense flavour. Amazing that once it was thought only fit as fodder for pigs. Lightly steamed, so that you keep in all of its goodness, and dressed with a hint of hazelnut oil, it is divine.'

In reality, most of the vegetables in the brassica group are likely to be just as good for you, since most are a source of sulforaphane. Brussels sprouts also have the beneficial compound sinigrin; and both of these

Most of the brassica group are rich in vitamins, minerals and antioxidants.

have been researched for their anti-cancer effects. For all their goodness, however, in terms of flavour, many members of the brassica group have long divided opinion, inspiring love or hatred, often depending on whether or not you were brought up on overcooked, unappetising offerings in the school canteen.

Sprouts have been the major culprit, and scientists discovered that an individual's reaction to them is less likely to be governed by a sad culinary experience than genetics. A particular gene governs the ability to taste the bitterness in the vegetable, but around half the world's population are thought to have a variance on the gene, which means they are unable to experience the bitterness in the same way and so are far more inclined to be sprout lovers. However, the image of the Brussels sprout has been greatly enhanced by the breeding and clever marketing of sweeter, tender and smaller varieties which no longer need the painstaking carving of crosses into their bases before cooking in order to allow the heat to penetrate through their tough stalks and tight balls of leaves. As a result, instead of being cooked into a grey, sodden mess, they are now more likely to be perkily crunchy in stir-fries or shredded raw into salads, and thanks to their sweeter flavour, the sprout-hating gene is less relevant.

Cabbages, too, have often inspired a love or hate reaction. 'But of all the brassicas,' says Raymond, 'cabbages were probably the most enjoyed and celebrated in our family, as they are in many cultures, because they are a cheap staple. The leaves might have been stuffed with forcemeat and simmered. Or fat chunks of cabbage would be put in a pot of water with smoked Morteau sausage and maybe some turnips, then they would simmer away, filling the whole house with smoky flavours. Heaven.'

Left: Upturned plant pots covering the tops of canes in the broccoli beds protect the gardener when working, and give a rustic look to the garden.

GROWING NOTES

GENERAL

Prepare beds in advance by digging in plenty of well-rotted manure or compost. Choose a sheltered, sunny site in the garden, with protection from the wind.

Although you can start off brassicas in a seed bed (see page 250) and then move them to their final destination, if you want to establish them a little more strongly first, sow them indoors in modules filled with compost: two seeds in each one. Cover with a fine layer of compost and water in.

Within a few weeks the seedlings will have emerged, and once they have two leaves, if both seeds have germinated, thin to just one seedling, snipping off the other at the base (don't be tempted to leave both, as they will compete with each other for nutrients and light). Once the thinned seedlings have reached four leaves, they are ready to be transferred to bigger individual pots (potting on). Make a hole in the centre of a pot of compost using a dibber (the pointed tool for making holes for seeds and bulbs) then push each module out from the base and lower into the hole. Firm in and water lightly.

Once the seedlings are established, plant them out into the prepared beds. Put in each plant and 'puddle in', i.e. fill each planting hole with water several times, letting it drain between each addition, then firm in with soil. This should ensure that the plants get plenty of moisture. After that just make sure that they are continually watered well, especially during dry spells.

Hoeing around the plants helps to keep the beds weed free.

All brassicas can be affected by cabbage root fly and cabbage caterpillar species (large cabbage white, small cabbage white and cabbage moth).

Cabbage root fly's white larvae are up to 2cm long and will eat the roots just below the surface of the soil, causing the plants to wilt and die. Brussels sprouts, cabbage and broccoli are especially prone to attacks by cabbage root fly (while kale is the most resilient) and biodegradable cabbage 'collars' which can be put around each stem offer the best protection.

'Cabbage caterpillars can decimate a crop,' says Alice. 'From late summer check every day for butterfly and moth eggs – they will lay them as close to their favourite food source as possible, and once hatched the caterpillars will make holes in the leaves and bore their way into the heart of the cabbage. Cover crops with butterfly netting, and if you see any eggs, remove them and squish them!'

Netting protects from pigeons, too, as they can also ruin a crop.

Clubroot is a disease that can affect all brassicas and cause them to become swollen, knobbly and twisted. If your soil is more alkaline than acidic, however, it should be less susceptible (the pH of your soil can be measured using a simple kit). You can spot the signs as the brassica leaves will usually become stunted and wilt. Once in the soil, the disease can live for a long time, so pull up the affected vegetables and destroy them (don't put them in the compost heap) and don't grow brassicas again in the same bed for at least six years.

BRUSSELS SPROUTS

Start off sowing seeds indoors in modules in April and pot on (see opposite).

Around June, when the young plants are 25cm high, transplant them to their permanent positions in the prepared beds.

Water the plants before moving, then plant in rows, leaving 60cm between each plant, and if you are growing in more than one row, leave a space of 75cm between each one. 'Puddle them in' (see opposite).

Start harvesting the sprouts by snapping them off from the bottom upwards, once they are the size of a walnut, firm, and their leaves are tightly closed. Although some varieties of sprout can be harvested as early as August it is generally considered that late varieties are best as the flavour is improved if the sprouts have been through a frost. This is because the plants accumulate a higher concentration of sugars in their cells to protect them from freezing, since the sugar solution, like antifreeze, has a lower freezing point.

CABBAGES

Spring cabbages (which are actually the hardiest of all) can be sown (see opposite) around August, potted on and then planted out in September so that they grow over winter and will be ready for harvest in April/May. Summer varieties are sown in February, planted out in April/May and harvested between May and July, while winter cabbages, including Savoy, can be sown from mid-May to early June, planted out in June/July, when they around 25cm high and harvested from late autumn onwards. Some varieties, such as Pyramid, are designed to be sown and harvested all year round.

'With some of the heritage varieties, germination can be much more sporadic than with modern hybrids which all come up together,' notes Alice. 'But there is something quite natural and beneficial about having cabbages that come up at different times, as you don't necessarily want them all at once.'

When you plant out, leave 45cm between each cabbage and 70cm between rows, and 'puddle them in' (see page 262).

Harvest by cutting through the stems with a sharp knife just above ground level.

KALE

Sow in June, pot on (see page 262) and then plant out in August, for harvesting between October and January, though you can begin cutting leaves from September on a cut-and-come-again basis, starting with the bigger outer leaves. If you want an earlier crop, you can sow earlier and harvest in the summer months, though some people say that kale tastes better if left in the ground until after the frost (see page 263).

PURPLE SPROUTING BROCCOLI

This stays in the ground for a long time using up space in the garden, however it gives you a good, nutritious leafy crop at a time when there is not a lot else around.

Sow in April, depending on the variety, pot on and then plant out into prepared beds (see page 262) around late May/early June.

Harvest throughout the following February, once you see the florets developing, and when the spears are around 15cm long. You should be able to harvest through to May, and if you keep picking you will hopefully encourage more spears to grow.

RAYMOND'S FLAVOUR NOTES

I love pointed summer cabbage cooked very quickly – I like the heritage French Oxheart and the modern variety, Caraflex. Winter Savoy is happy cooked at high or low temperatures.

For salads, the crunchy red cabbage is lovely finely chopped with a tiny bit of oil. Scatter over a few sautéed lardons if you like.

All brassicas are at their most nutritious within 48 hours of being harvested and eaten raw, or lightly steamed, as some cooking methods may reduce their goodness. When the vegetables are freshly picked and bitten into, or chopped, enzymes get to work on a group of substances in cruciferous vegetables known as glucosinolates – these are sulphur-containing chemicals that give the characteristic pungent aroma and bitter flavour. As a result, the glucosinolates break down into a number of compounds, including the all-important sulforaphane. Cooking, however, may shut down this enzyme activity. My partner Natalia, a doctor and expert on nutrition, explains that one way to counteract this if you are going to cook brassicas, is to let them sit for a few minutes once you have chopped them, in order to maximise the enzyme activity before cooking.

PURPLE SPROUTING BROCCOLI AND POACHED EGG

This is a wonderful, simple dish based around just two ingredients, each completely delicious, and each holding a very high nutritional profile. Yet these components – the purple sprouting broccoli and the poached egg – need to be cooked to perfection. The technique used here, which I have used for so many of the vegetables in this book, steams the broccoli and not only helps to conserve its nutrients, it also helps retain a wonderful crunchy bite.

SERVES 4

Preparation time: 5 minutes
Cooking time: 5 minutes

For the poached eggs
1 litre water
40ml white wine vinegar (see
   Cook's note)
4 eggs

For the purple sprouting broccoli
50ml water
10g unsalted butter
2 tsp sea salt
12 purple sprouting broccoli
   spears

To serve
20g hazelnuts, toasted and
   crushed
2 chive sprigs, finely chopped
20g Pata Negra de Bellota ham,
   sliced crossways (optional)

For poaching the eggs, have ready four small ramekins and line a tray with kitchen paper. Place a medium shallow pan on a medium heat with the litre of water and vinegar. Bring to a boil then leave at a gentle simmer.

For the purple sprouting broccoli, in a small saucepan place the water, butter and a tiny pinch of salt.

Crack the perfectly fresh eggs into the ramekins. Slide each egg into the water and barely simmer for $3\frac{1}{2}$ minutes.

While the eggs are poaching, bring the broccoli water to a full boil and 'steam' the tender spears, covered with a lid, for no more than 3 minutes.

Using a slotted spoon, carefully lift the eggs from the water and place on the lined tray. Repeat for the broccoli.

To serve, reheat the hazelnuts in a dry pan on a medium heat. Spoon the steaming-hot purple sprouting broccoli on to serving plates. With a slotted spoon, add the eggs. Scatter over the hazelnuts, chopped chives and the ham, if using.

Cook's note
The vinegar helps to coagulate and gather the egg white around the yolk.

KALE WITH SWEET AND SOUR PORK BELLY AND QUINCE PUREE

I recently tasted a variety of kale we have been growing in the garden at Kew, called Westland Winter, and was absolutely amazed by its flavour. Iron-rich and just a little bitter, yet balanced with the hint of sweetness that comes from the first frost, it was begging to be used in a recipe. I've cooked it very quickly and simply to retain its powerhouse of nutrients (see page 258); it's a perfect partner to the succulent, gently spiced pork belly.

SERVES 4

Preparation time: 20 minutes
Cooking time: 3½ hours

For the sweet and sour pork belly
70g acacia or Manuka honey
50g tomato ketchup
2 tbsp light soy sauce
4 tsp rice wine vinegar
10g root ginger, peeled and finely diced
½ red chilli, deseeded and finely diced
¼ shallot, finely diced
75g large quince (about¼), peeled and cut into 2cm wedges
500g pork belly, all bones and skin removed, skin scored

For the kale
100ml water
20g butter
pinch sea salt
280g Westland Winter or Red Curled kale leaves
8 Nero di Toscana kale leaves

To serve
150g Quince Purée (see page 278)
1 tbsp sesame seeds, lightly toasted

Preheat the oven to 120°C/Gas Mark ½.

For the pork belly, in a medium casserole with a lid, mix all the ingredients except the pork, then add the belly and baste the sauce over the top. Transfer to the oven for 3 hours, basting the sauce over the pork every 20 minutes. When cooked, the pork will be firm but offer little resistance when a knife is inserted. Remove from the oven, lift the pork out of the casserole and place to one side to rest, loosely covered with foil.

Strain the cooking juices into a medium saucepan on a high heat and bring to a boil. Reduce the liquid by half so that it thickly coats the back of a spoon. Remove from the heat and reserve.

To cook the kale, in a large saucepan, bring the water, butter and salt to the boil. Add both varieties of kale and cook, covered, for 3–4 minutes, until barely cooked but still retaining a bit of bite and their wonderful colour. Strain.

To serve, spread a spoonful of the quince purée in the centre of each plate. Add the kale, slice the pork belly and divide between the plates. Finish with a little of the reduced cooking juices and scatter over the sesame seeds.

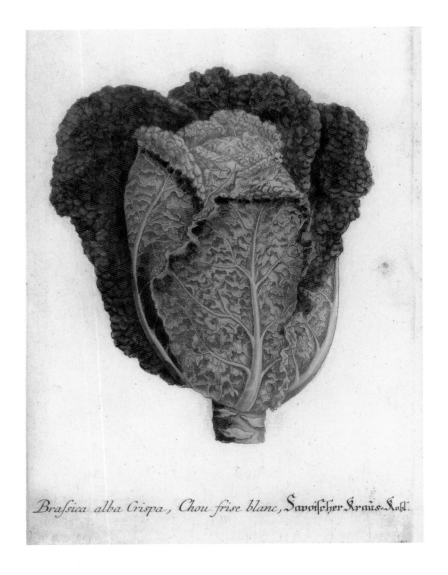

Brassica alba Crispa, Chou frise blanc, Savoischer Kraus-Kohl.

Left: Brassica alba Crispa, *as it was then known, a variety of* Brassica oleracea *(Savoy cabbage), from* Phytanthoza iconographia, *vol. 1: t.262 (1737) by German apothecary and botanist Johann Wilhelm Weinmann. The work, over eight volumes, contains over 1,000 hand-coloured engravings.*

QUINCE

'SOME PEOPLE SAY THAT IT WASN'T AN APPLE that Eve ate in the Garden of Eden, but a quince. I am not a historian, but with my cook's hat on, I have to say I doubt that very much,' says Raymond. 'Have you ever tried to bite into a raw quince? You would most likely lose all your teeth. Adam would look at Eve and say, "no way!"'

In Victorian times quince was a regular feature of the walled garden.

The Garden of Eden story may be one step too far, but this most ancient of fruits, originally native to the Caucasus mountains of Iran and Armenia, has enjoyed a seductive image in many cultures. The Greeks, in particular, saw the fruit as a symbol of love, marriage and fertility.

'I have always loved quince,' says Raymond. 'Not only its rich flavour and perfume, but there is such a strong sexuality about it that completely captures my imagination. Around early November, when the heavy fruits are starting to turn from green to yellow, they have a fine down over their skin, and they seem to me to be taut, rippled balls of muscle – very masculine. But then you cut through the hard, granular flesh – you need a big, strong, heavy knife to do it – and inside the fruit is completely female, full of almost-ripe seeds. It's extraordinary.'

The Romans preserved quince in a syrup of boiled-down grape juice (must) and honey, an ancient precursor of the fruit paste known as 'cheese' in England and 'membrillo' in Portugal and Spain. Quince jams were also the forerunners of marmalade, whose name comes from the Portuguese word for quince, *marmelo*. In medieval times, when the feasting at noble and royal tables featured a mixture of sweet and savoury dishes, quince was a favourite, along with other fruits, nuts and spices; and by Victorian times most walled gardens would have had a quince tree or two, and the fruit would have been served with roasted game and other meats, or made into jellies, jams and puddings.

Over the years, as other more easily prepared fruits became readily available, quince began to fall out of favour and many trees and orchards disappeared. Now, though, along with a thirst for rediscovering heritage varieties of the quince's relatives, the apple and pear, this most evocative of fruits is making a long overdue comeback.

GROWING NOTES

You can buy established quince trees in a variety of sizes, from large orchard ones to smaller bushier ones that can be grown in pots on patios or in small gardens. Quince can also be trained in a fan shape against a sunny wall. Vranja is a favourite of Raymond's and well suited to growing in the British climate.

They are best bought as two-year-old trees, however they won't start producing a crop until they are about five years old.

If planting in the garden, put the trees in between November and March in a sunny position and mulch around the base with well-rotted manure or compost to help keep the moisture in the soil.

Keep watered in dry spells – quince trees like moist, yet well-draining soils.

Keep weed free around the base of the trunk.

In wet weather, trees can be prone to quince leaf blight, a fungal disease that causes the leaves to become spotted and misshapen and often fall off the tree too early. To stop the disease from carrying over to the next season, dispose of any infected leaves and prune out dead shoots in winter.

The other problem that can beset quince is brown rot – also a fungal disease, which, as it suggests, causes brown rot, as well as white fungal spores on the fruit. 'Any wounds to the flesh, including those made by birds and squirrels, provide the perfect point for infection to begin', says Joe, 'so covering the trees with netting can help. Make sure you dispose of any

affected fruit straight away, to prevent the rot from spreading.'

The fruit is ready to harvest around October/November time, when it has turned from pale yellow to a deep golden – it will also be very aromatic. Handle carefully to avoid bruising.

Only harvest the undamaged fruit, as the quinces need to be 'bletted', i.e. stored without touching each other in shallow, well-ventilated wooden boxes, in a cool, dark, dry place for six weeks so that they mature.

In winter, when the tree is dormant, remove any of the 'three Ds' that you find: 'dead, damaged or diseased' branches. Aim to prune each tree into a neat shape focusing on about six main branches which have small sub-branches growing from them. Cut back the ends of the main branches by about a third, to allow a good circulation of air, which always helps to keep disease at bay.

RAYMOND'S FLAVOUR NOTES

I love quince, but the granular nature of its flesh, which takes so long to soften, means that working with it (other than to make it into jelly and jam), has always posed a problem. Now, though, I have found the variety, Vranja, that makes the difference – big and pear shaped, its texture is softer, creamier and it can be cooked faster.

Right: Quince, Cydonia vulgaris, *from* Flora von Deutschland *by Otto Wilhelm Thomé (1840-1925), vol.3, plate 419. Illustrated by Walter Müller.*

POACHED QUINCE AND WINTER FRUIT IN SPICED WINE

Quince are a truly magnificent fruit. In fact, I love them so much that I've planted four trees in my restaurant's garden, one in front of each kitchen window. I find their beauty ravishing – delicate white flowers against a dark wintery backdrop, broad leaves and soft, downy fruit.

For me, making this dessert defines an exact moment in the season – the end of autumn and the beginning of winter – and it's one I'll prepare as soon as the first quince are ripe. However, with its warm and spicy flavours it is also a lovely prelude to Christmas. I know that blackberries don't grow in winter but they freeze well and I hope that you might have collected a few on long autumn walks in the brambles and frozen them to use throughout the winter. They'll add a wonderful burst of juiciness to your crumbles, tarts and poached fruits.

I would normally use a vanilla purée but here I want the vanilla flavour to diffuse its flavour slowly so as to penetrate the quince and the most effective means of achieving this is to use a pod.

SERVES 4

Preparation time: 20 minutes, plus
　　freezing
Cooking time: 35 minutes

For the red wine jus
400ml red wine (see Chef's note)
400ml water
2 tsp stevia powder or 100g caster
　　sugar
½ vanilla pod
4 small cinnamon sticks
2 black peppercorns
2 bay leaves
2 cloves
2 thin slices lemon
2 thin slices orange

For the winter fruit
2 quince, peeled, cored and
　　quartered
2 Cox's Orange Pippin apples,
　　peeled, cored and quartered
2 very ripe Conference pears,
　　peeled and quartered
handful frozen blackberries
4 Agen prunes

For the red wine jus, in a saucepan on a high heat, bring the red wine to the boil for 2 minutes, which will remove much of the alcohol, then add the water and the remaining ingredients and bring to a gentle simmer.

To poach the fruit, first add the quince to the simmering jus and poach for around 25 minutes. Then add the apple and the pear and continue to simmer for 4 minutes. Take off the heat, add the blackberries and leave to cool to room temperature before adding the prunes. Strain a third of the liquor and freeze overnight; transfer the remainder to the fridge.

To serve, remove the frozen cooking liquor from the freezer and scrape with a fork to create beautiful flakes of perfumed ice. Arrange all the fruit, spices, red wine and cooking juices in a large dish or divide between four bowls. At the last moment, take a spoonful of the delicate flakes of spiced wine granita and serve on top of your dessert. You could also serve the granita in small cups from the freezer as a little pre-dessert.

Chef's notes
My general rule about wine when cooking is not to use an expensive bottle. You are looking for a deep, rich-coloured Cabernet Sauvignon or Merlot. Pinot Noir is too light.

It is important that the liquid does not boil while poaching the fruits as the intensity of the heat will damage their delicate flesh.

QUINCE PUREE

This is a versatile purée that can be served hot or cold and works perfectly for either sweet or savoury dishes. I've served it with my Sweet and Sour Pork Belly (see page 268) but I'll happily eat it for breakfast with natural yoghurt and toasted oats.

MAKES around 500g

Preparation time: 5 minutes
Cooking time: 10 minutes

For the quince purée
300ml water
100ml dry white wine
1 tsp Vanilla Purée (see page 281)
    or good-quality vanilla extract
40g stevia powder
4 quince, peeled, deseeded and
    segmented

In a large saucepan on a medium heat, bring the water, wine, vanilla purée or extract and stevia to the boil. Add the quince, cover with a lid and cook for 10 minutes on a gentle simmer. Remove from the heat and blend to a fine purée in a blender or using a hand-held blender.

Variation
You can choose not to blend the cooked quince and simply store them in the chilled cooking liquor. They are perfect to keep as bottled fruit in a sealed jar for up to two weeks.

BASIC RECIPES
Brown chicken stock

A homemade stock is the simplest way I know to add a touch of magic to your sauces. I created this chicken stock about 40 years ago and it has remained practically unchanged since then. It has several merits: it is relatively cheap and the stock is well flavoured with a good colour. Most importantly it will not take up hours of your time. Of course making stock is not as easy as dissolving a cube in water, but the results are not comparable and are well worth the effort.

MAKES: 1.1 litres

Preparation time: 5 minutes
Cooking time: 2½ hours

3kg chicken wings, chopped into
    3cm pieces
1kg turkey bones, chopped into
    3cm pieces
200g duck fat
2.2 litres cold water
200g white onion (about 1),
    roughly chopped
100g carrots, roughly chopped
50g celery (about 1 stick), roughly
    chopped
6 garlic cloves, skin on, crushed
250g field mushrooms, sliced 5mm
    thick
6g dried trompettes, roughly
    chopped (optional)
1 bay leaf
2 thyme sprigs
20 black peppercorns

Preheat the oven to 220°C/Gas Mark 7.

Place the chicken and turkey pieces on to three oven trays, pour over the duck fat and with a large wooden spoon, stir the bones in the fat so they are evenly coated. The duck fat will not only bring its own flavour to the roasting process but it will also roast at a higher temperature, giving you a better colour which will result in more flavour.

Roast in the oven for 20 minutes. Stir the meat with a wooden spoon and continue to roast for a further 20 minutes, stir once again and cook for a final 10 minutes, until you have an even golden brown colour all over. You will need to swap the top and bottom tray over halfway through cooking to ensure an even distribution of heat and caramelisation.

While the browned meat is still hot, drain off all the fat and reserve 50ml of the fat for cooking the vegetables; the rest can be stored in the fridge for future use.

With a slotted spoon, transfer the browned bones to a large stock pot. On a medium heat, deglaze the roasting trays with a little of the cold water and scrape all the meat sediments which have gathered at the bottom of the tray with a wooden spoon, add this to the stock pot of browned bones. This will provide more flavour and colour to your stock.

In a separate large sauté pan on a high heat, fry the onion, carrots, celery and garlic in the 50ml of strained duck fat until caramelised. Add the sliced mushrooms, dried trompettes, if using, and cook for 2 minutes, until they have softened. Add the vegetables to the stock pot along with the herbs, peppercorns and remaining cold water. The water should barely cover the bones. Bring to the boil, skim and simmer gently for 1½ hours. It is important that you use cold water and bring your stock to the boil as this will lift all the impurities and fats to the surface, making it easier to skim with a ladle; so you obtain a clear stock. Do not stir the stock or you will make it cloudy. Strain the stock and reserve. I never use any salt in any of my meat stocks; the meat has its own richness and also contains a small amount of salt. The stock can be kept in the fridge for up to five days or frozen for a month.

Chef's note

I have chopped the poultry bones into small pieces to obtain the maximum surface area coloration, giving me more colour, more flavour and reducing the cooking time to obtain a very fresh stock.

Using turkey bones as well as chicken bones gives the stock extra wholesomeness.

Vanilla purée

Vanilla is part of the orchid family and Kew has the largest collection of orchids in the world. Vanilla is also the second most expensive spice after saffron.

Vanilla is so often just infused in milk and then discarded; this recipe will use 95 per cent of the vanilla. You can also store the purée for a long time, up to a month, and create magic when you taste your vanilla cream – little starbursts of vanilla particles pop in your mouth, adding another layer of texture to the taste.

You will know when you have a good vanilla pod when you roll it between your fingers. 'She' should be soft and full and you can feel she is pregnant with millions of seeds. Never buy a hard, dried pod.

MAKES: 300 ml

100ml water
100g caster sugar
4 vanilla pods, finely chopped

In a heavy-bottomed pan over a medium heat, mix the water and sugar and bring to the boil, then cool. When the syrup is barely warm, throw in all the vanilla pieces.

Blend in a blender for 4–5 minutes, until the vanilla is completely broken down into a fine, silken purée. Then pour it into a small sterilised jar with a screwtop lid or kilner jar.

The purée can be kept refrigerated for up to a month. Its sugar content is about 60 per cent, and as sugar is a preservative it will keep the vanilla from deteriorating.

INDEX

Note: pages numbers in **bold** refer to information in captions.

Raymond Blanc and the publishers would like to thank:

At Kew: Richard Deverell, Director; Richard Barley, Director of Horticulture; Gina Fullerlove, Head of Publishing; Richard Wilford, Head of Gardens Design and Collections Support; Martin Staniforth, Acting Principal, School of Horticulture; Mark Nesbitt, Economic Botany Manager; Melanie-Jayne Howes, Pharmacist, Sustainable Uses of Plants Group; Monique Simmonds, Deputy Director of Science; Ruth Eastwood, Crop Wild Relatives Project Co-ordinator; Paula Rudall, Head of Comparative Plant and Fungal Biology; Lynn Parker, Art Collections Curator; archival photographer Paul Little; and gardeners Alice Lumb and Joe Archer.

Raymond's team: Anna Greenland, Head Vegetable Gardener; Anne-Marie Owens, Head Gardener; Adam Johnson, Head Development Chef; Ben Howarth, Assistant Development Chef; Lydia Shevell, Business Director; Natalia Traxel, MD, Pg. Dip Applied Human Nutrition; Leanda Pearman, PA to Raymond Blanc; Tracie Davies, Assistant PA to Raymond Blanc and Rosemary Scoular at United Agents.

At Lion TV: Richard Bradley, Managing Director; Donna Clark, Executive Producer, Giulia Clark, Series Producer; Stuart Elliott, Series Director; Emma Randle-Caprez and Georgina Stewart, Assistant Producers; Claire Smith, Production Manager; Laura Rawlinson, photographer; Susan Cooke, Director of Legal; and Julian Alexander at LAW Agency.

At the BBC: Alison Kirkham, Janice Hadlow, Tanya Shaw and Kim Shillinglaw.

Susanne Groom, former curator at Historic Royal Palaces; and Janet Oldroyd-Hulme, Yorkshire Rhubarb specialist.

Jean Cazals, David Eldridge at Two Associates, Sheila Keating and Imogen Fortes.

This book is published to accompany the television series entitled *Kew on a Plate*, first broadcast on BBC Two in 2015.

Executive Producer for the BBC: Alison Kirkham
Executive Producer for Lion TV: Donna Clark
Text © Lion Television Ltd 2015
Recipes © Raymond Blanc 2015
Illustrations © Board of Trustees of the Royal Botanic Gardens, Kew
Recipe and still life photography © Jean Cazals 2015
Garden photography © Jean Cazals 2015 except pages 2, 10, 16 (top), 22 (bottom), 27 (top), 56, 59, 71–75, 116–17, 129, 147, 203 (top), 207 (bottom), 263–4 Lion Television Ltd; pages 45, 89, 118, 192–3, 203 (bottom), 222, 240–1 Joe Archer; pages 8, 27 (bottom), 176, 193, 207 (top) Anna Greenland
Format and Programme Material © Lion Television Ltd

First published in 2015 by HEADLINE PUBLISHING GROUP

Cataloguing in Publication Data is available from the British Library

Hardback ISBN 9781472224378

Project editor: Imogen Fortes
Design: Two Associates
Recipe and still life photography: Jean Cazals
Prop styling: Pene Parker
Garden reportage photography: Jean Cazals, Laura Rawlinson, Joe Archer and Anna Greenland
Recipe development and food styling: Adam Johnson, Head Development Chef to Raymond Blanc; Ben Howarth, Assistant Development Chef to Raymond Blanc

All botanical illustrations are taken from the Library, Art and Archives Collections of the Royal Botanic Gardens, Kew.
Art Collections Curator: Lynn Parker
Kew Archive Photographer: Paul Little

Photograph of Richard Barley by Georgina Barley
Photographs on page 40 by N. Hulme

Printed and bound by Mohn Media

HEADLINE PUBLISHING GROUP
An Hachette UK Company
338 Euston Road
London NW1 3BH
www.headline.co.uk
www.hachette.co.uk

ROYAL BOTANIC GARDENS

RAYMOND BLANC

www.raymondblanc.com

television

an all3media company